ISSUES FOR THE SEVENTIES

AMERICANIZATION

ISSUES FOR THE SEVENTIES

AMERICANIZATION

EDITED BY

HUGH INNIS

Ryerson Polytechnical Institute, Toronto, Ontario

CONSULTING EDITOR: Norman Sheffe

McGRAW-HILL RYERSON LIMITED

Toronto   Montreal   New York   London   Sydney
  Johannesburg   Mexico   Panama   Düsseldorf
Singapore   Rio de Janeiro   Kuala Lumpur   New Delhi

ISSUES FOR THE SEVENTIES

AMERICANIZATION

ISBN   0-07-092943-2

3456789   AP72   98765

Printed and bound in Canada

CONTENTS

ACKNOWLEDGEMENTS

Cover and page 28: Courtesy Standard Oil Company (N.J.).
Distributed by Imperial Oil Limited
Cover and page 46: Bob Brooks from Miller Services
Cover and page 87: Fred Phipps from Miller Services
Page 4: Reprinted with permission *Toronto Daily Star*
Page 15: From Miller Services
Page 53: NFB from Miller Services

INTRODUCTION

One historian has called Canada and the United States "the Siamese twins of North America who cannot separate and live." It is difficult to imagine what life would be like in Canada without our many connections with the United States. Our relationship is a wrap-around one. In addition to official connections between governments there is a vast mosaic of personal, social, and cultural relationships between the two countries.

We belong to innumerable associations of various kinds which have contacts in the United States, from Kiwanis to Junior League to Y.M.C.A. We work for American companies and belong to American labour unions. And what Canadian does not have a friend or relative in the United States?

There are many cultural contacts between us, and because the U.S.A.'s population is so much bigger than Canada's, these often seem to be one-way contacts. We read American books and magazines and watch American television and movies.

In the face of so many connections to the United States, are we clear in our minds about what Canada is? What a Canadian is? Are Americans and Canadians different? Do we want to remain different?

Ever since 1775, when the Americans broke away from Britain and attacked Montreal, we have had a love-hate relationship with United States. At times we have seemed to envy their kind of open political system; at other times we have called it mob rule. We both fear their emotionalism and are drawn to it. We are both delighted and appalled by the United States, often simultaneously. So conscious are we of the presence and power of our big neighbour that the nationalism of Canadian people often seems anti-American rather than pro-Canadian.

Like the attack on Canada in 1775, the war of 1812 was an attempt by the Americans to injure England by attacking her northern colonies. These attacks were not successful, and they helped to form a distinctive Canadian nationalism which is still very much alive. Nevertheless, in 1849 we were ready to join the Americans, when the British stopped giving us trade privileges. In 1854 we signed a trade treaty with the U.S.A., but by the late 1860s the British were supporting the southern states in the Civil War and the northern states were unhappy with Canada. There were several unsuccessful attempts to establish strong trading treaties between the two countries in the late 19th and early 20th centuries, and today the great preponderance of our trade, both export and import, is with the U.S.A. What is more, Americans are now the largest investors in Canadian resources, industry, and business.

Between 1914 and 1945, Canada came to maturity as an industrial nation but, ironically, the qualifications for mature nationhood have changed in the post-war period. Manufacturing production now works on such a large scale that a market of 20 million people is not big enough to satisfy the latest technology. Thus, in Europe the "common market" countries have formed an economic unit, and Canada seems pushed by necessity into ever closer economic arrangements with United States. Moreover, self-defence by small nations is no longer possible. To defend herself, therefore, Canada has joined the United States in schemes for continental defence.

Canada finds herself a nation at a time when events seem to have significantly changed the meaning of the word.

H. I.

Part 1

The industrial and economic and financial penetration from the south worries me, but less than the penetration of American ideas, of the flow of information about all things American; American thoughts and entertainment; the American approach to everything.

Lester Pearson

NATIONAL IDENTITY

F. R. Scott

Frank Scott is a poet and teacher of law who has been very active in the area of civil rights. He lives in Montreal.

The Canadian Centenary Council
Meeting in Le Reine Elizabeth
To seek those symbols
Which will explain ourselves to
    ourselves
Evoke unlimited responses
And prove that something called
    Canada
Really exists in the hearts of all

Reprinted with permission of F. R. Scott.

Handed out to every delegate
At the start of proceedings
A portfolio of documents
On the cover of which appeared
In gold letters
          not
A Mari Usque Ad Mare
          not
E Pluribus Unum
          not
Dieu et Mon Droit
          not
Je me souviens
          but
"Courtesy of Coca-Cola Limited."

CANADIAN STATEHOOD

Paul Rush

Paul Rush is Managing Editor of Week end Magazine.

The Time: somewhere in the not-too-distant future.

The Place: Ottawa (or Ottawashington, as some call it).

The Occasion: celebration of Canadian statehood.

The Speaker: the governor of the great state of Canada.

It gives me great pleasure to be with you today in joint observance of this glorious holiday. A holiday, I might add, that shows our pride in our heritage.

As you know, last year by an act of our legislature — and it is with pride I say *our* legislature — the first Monday in July is marked as Canada Day, a day which everyone in this great state may be proud of. Proud because this is a decision we took ourselves. And it is this decision that I feel sure marks us Canadians as a state not like the others.

But it is not our decisiveness alone that marks us. Oh, no. We are second in population only to California, and perhaps New York. (I fear I forgot about New York there.) We are larger than Alaska. Larger than Texas and Alaska put together. We are rich in resources. So rich that we happily share with our fellows. We are the playground of these glorious 51 states. Our fellow Americans flock here to see the famous Calgary Stampede, the Canadian State Fair, the changing of the state police at our magnificent legislature in Ottawa. And many love to visit the quaint little city of Quebec where some of the ancient traditions and the . . . er, French language have been so carefully preserved.

But it is not these things of which I come here before you to speak. No, my friends, I come here to attack. Yes, attack a small band of willful men who would tear us out of this fruitful union, this union that has seen us achieve our true destiny. I might even venture to say our manifest destiny.

Let me categorize these enemies. For truly, by their sins ye shall know them.

First: the Gordonites. It is true that this sect has been largely discredited and is found only on isolated university campuses. But, I warn you, they preach a sinister brand of, yes, let me say it, nationalism. They would have us turn back the clock, discard our advantages, our cars, our color TV sets, our cherished institutions such as the National Guard. They would plunge us into the dark ages, restore the borders that hemmed us in many

Reprinted with permission of *Weekend Magazine,* by Paul Rush, from the issue of June 27, 1970.

years ago. They would cut our standard of living in half. They seek to make us self-sufficient. We, whose markets are with our fellow states. They would have us process our own raw materials. We, with our tradition of letting our fellow states do the processing. I urge you, in your pride as Canadians, remember our traditions and ignore their siren song.

Second: the Juneauites. These too, and few they are, are found only in the poorer districts of our larger cities where they preach the preservation of our culture. Culture indeed. Our culture is wedded to that of our fellow states. Do we not speak the same tongue, have the same interests, share the same goals, watch the same TV programs? I urge you, in your pride, remember our great traditions and ignore these people. And here, I think I may add, I have it on good authority that we may be permitted a team in the National Hockey League when it expands this fall to Butte, Texarkana, Greensboro, Bakersville and Topeka.

Third: the Québecois. (I hope I pronounced that correctly.) I realize that few of you may realize that these people still exist but there are scattered bands who still meet and preach a return to those quaint days of yore. They have the ridiculous idea that we can be made a "nation", a nation mind you, with two main languages, English and French. Of all the ridiculous ideas. They preach that we will find strength in diversity. Their ideas have long been discredited and we have found strength in assimilation — or, should I say union. I urge you, in your pride as Canadians, remember our tradition as a united people and ignore those who would throw you back into the past.

Fourth: the royalists. Again, I am embarrassed to talk about something so antiquated. So, let me say, medi-aeval. These people are still found on the west coast, singing their ridiculous songs and prating of kings and queens. They would restore the Union Jack and have us discard our beautiful Stars and Stripes. They would take Washington off the dollar, Lincoln off the penny. They would dishonor the founders of our great nation and restore the yoke of imperialism. I urge you, in your pride as Canadians, to ignore these poor deluded people.

Fifth, and last, the conservationists. This is a heresy that has come and gone and come again. It preaches something that we, as enlightened citizens, can only regard as unnatural. Consider for a minute. They would shut down our mines and mills that we depend on. They say we should preserve the water and the forest. And for what? For pleasure, that's what. Selfish pleasure. They would have us forget our duty to our fellow man. I say to you, water is made for man and man must use it in his industry. They would have us swim in lakes and river water. Imagine, swimming in lakes and rivers when we have these lovely swimming pools! They would restore the forests and bring back wild beasts to live in them. Have you ever heard of anything so ridiculous as bringing back bears and wolves and deer? Why, you might as well bring back the buffalo! You might as well bring back the Eskimo! I ask you, have we not museums enough and zoos enough where our children can study the remnants of the past that so long shackled us? I urge you to ignore these people as you should ignore all the rest.

I am sorry to have brought up these items at this time when our minds are concerned with the celebration of our glorious heritage but I assure you that my words are consistent with great traditions. We come from a long line of patriots, Paul Revere, Thomas Jefferson, Abraham Lincoln, Theodore Roosevelt, Harry Truman, Richard Nixon. As a key part of these United States we carry forth our heritage to the world around us and we must be true to what we believe in. That is why I speak as I do. That is why I warn you of those who would undermine us.

But enough. Let us close this speech with our national anthem. Fellow Canadians, I ask you to join me:

"'Oh, say can you see . . .'"

CANADA AND U.S. (1)
There's a Profound Difference

Howard Lentner

Howard Lentner is Chairman of the Department of Political Science at McMaster University in Hamilton.

The United States and Canada appear, at first glance, to be more similar than different. An American moving from industrial mid-America to industrial Ontario suffers little more culture shock than he would if he were to move from Pittsburgh to Chicago, and his Canadian counterpart has a similar experience. Yet, when he examines the two countries in more detail, he finds that these appearances mask real differences.

Relative rather than gross, the differences are nevertheless substantial. They stem from the different origins and histories of the two countries. Constitutions and geography, society and institutions, and other factors — contemporary and past — all have helped to shape today's results. One finds many differences in the panorama of the past, and one sees differences today.

Are these differences only superficial? Are the differences only those of wealth and size and age, with Canada but a few years behind developments in the United States? Or are Canadians different from Americans in some characteristic and profound way?

Individual and society

I believe there is a central difference between the two peoples. This central difference has to do with the relationship of the individual to society. In the United States, social groups make greater demands on the individual than do equivalent groups in Canada; and individuals in the United States commit themselves to fulfilling group expectations with more intense activity and enthusiasm than do their Canadian counterparts. These are profound characteristics.

To see this is to gain clarity of insight into the two cultures, and this gives us a perspective from which to view the current problem of American influence in Canada.

Reprinted with the permission of the author, from *Toronto Daily Star*, August, 19, 1970.

The immense problems today in the United States of cities, race and war make that country very unattractive to many Canadians. Viewing the growth of American influence in Canada—particularly cultural and economic influence — many Canadians wonder whether they can preserve their way of life against unwanted influence.

If a people is formed by its experiences, then the forging of its unity and independence is the first and perhaps most profound common heritage.

There are sharp contrasts in the origins of the United States and Canada. The United States conducted the first modern revolution at the end of the 18th century. It was fought against what was regarded as British tyranny and on behalf of freedom. Canada forced its unity by a conference on confederation in the mid-19th century, the founders carefully keeping in mind the civil war that had recently ended in the United States. Canadian independence was achieved gradually, culminating in the 20th century, and even then not rejecting the British crown. Although both countries are fragments of the British empire, their rejection of colonial status took such different forms that the contrast is very sharp.

Sense of confidence

The revolution gave Americans a sense of confidence in themselves that has been apparent throughout their history. The rejection of tyranny carried with it Jefferson's distrust of government and reliance on the individual to control his own destiny. Confidence and distrust — these are contradictory thrusts of the American character that have been held simultaneously throughout American history. To take just one example, at the same time that Americans were accepting Jack-

son's version of egalitarian democracy, they were also developing the doctrine of manifest destiny which carried the implication that a strong government would seek to fill out a continent.

The impact of origins on Canadians has been very different. Not explicitly rejecting tyranny, they have not developed the same distrust of government. Not having forged their confidence in the fires of revolution, they have not sought a destiny.

This difference is perhaps best illustrated in the contrasting ways in which the two nations opened and settled their frontiers. Americans, relying on individual initiative and providing an outlet for those citizens who did not conform to the civilization of the eastern seaboard, opened up and settled the frontier as families and small groups, without the benefit of the central government. They paid the price of such immense liberty for the individual in going through a period without the order and justice that can be brought only by authority.

Canadians, on the other hand, settled their frontiers by first sending the national police to bring about a structure of authority and order. Only then did the citizen-settlers move to the vast mid-continental spaces to take up new lives. There was perhaps less adventure and less material for Hollywood, but they never gave up the civilization that government brings.

Neither country has lost that valuable part of its British heritage of constitutional government and democratic mechanisms for controlling authority. Nevertheless, the attitudes of the two peoples have been quite different towards authority, and Canadians seem to have resolved the ancient tension between freedom and order while Americans have preserved the tension.

There has been and is a much

heavier British influence in Canada than in the United States. In Canada, the monarchy has been preserved; governmental institutions closely emulate those of the British; American colonists who remained loyal to Britain in the revolution emigrated in large numbers to Canada; and there are myriad traces of other influences from Britain. This greater influence of Britain continues despite the existence of French Canada.

Federal systems

Both the United States and Canada have federal systems, but there the similarity ends. The United States may be characterized certainly in the 20th century, as moving in the direction of centralization. The states have lost considerable power relative to the national government. The trend has gone so far that analysts as often refer to the national government as to the federal government. Canada, on the other hand, has been the subject of growing power in the provinces, and one almost never hears a reference in Canada to the national government: it is always referred to as the federal government.

Two fundamental characteristics seem to explain most of these developments: the relative sizes of the provinces and the states, and the existence of Quebec.

Most of the provinces are much larger than the states. The strength of such an immense province as Ontario with respect to the federal government makes the strength of even a very powerful state, such as New York or California, seem pale by comparison.

The existence of Quebec with its separate language and culture is unlike anything in the United States. It is impossible for federal authorities not to take account of a province when its presence is so obviously there

and when even federal programs must be structured with the French fact in mind. And all 10 provinces have benefitted by this unique character of Quebec. Without that character, the entire evolution of federalism in Canada would probably have been quite different, and probably it would have moved in a centralizing direction.

Provinces interfered

In World War I, Canada made approximately the same absolute sacrifices as did the United States, and in World War II, Canada made approximately the same relative sacrifices as did the United States. But, in both wars, Canada was prevented, largely by Quebec, from mobilizing the total nation for a total war effort. In all of the influences in Canada which have driven the United States to centralization, Canada's provinces have interfered.

The centralizing influences have not been so strong in Canada as in the United States. Not being of great power status, Canada has not been moved to adopt a powerful military establishment or to increase the federal executive power in conducting foreign relations. Although Canada has been a participant in the North Atlantic Treaty Organization, it has not had peacetime conscription. The element of official secrecy associated with national security policy has not become an important factor in Canada; thus Canadians have been spared the increase of executive power that flows from it.

Canada, of course, has been subject to the more general movement of the 20th century which has seen a shift of relative power from legislatures to executives. In some ways, the constitutional arrangements make the government a more powerful influence in Canada than the executive in the

United States. With disciplined parties in a parliamentary system, the government introduces a bill which one can expect will become law. In contrast, when the American president sends a bill to Congress, one can expect that the bill will not survive intact. In short, without the hindrances of the American checks and balances system, the Canadian government has the ability to govern effectively. This general proposition applies also to the provincial governments.

CANADA AND U.S. (2)
Mosaic, Melting Pot — both myths

Howard Lentner

The people of both Canada and the United States have long been dominated by those segments of their respective societies which are derived from English patrimony. Because Canada has clung more closely than the Unied States to the culture of their common ancestry, there are subtle differences in class structure and deference patterns.

Both countries, however, have drawn major segments of their populations from throughout Europe, with a sprinkling of population from Asia. Although their respective myths for absorbing these non-English people differ, there appears to be no significant difference in the patterns of integration into the respective societies.

The American myth of the melting pot has concentrated on weaving non-English-speaking minorities into the fabric of the dominant culture, but there continues to be a minority language press, and one can find distinct neighborhoods which are outposts of non-English European and Asian culture. These neighborhoods continue to exist into the second and third generations.

Similar patterns

In mythological but not practical contrast, Canada has clung to the idea of the mosaic society in which non-dominant cultures are encouraged to survive. Despite the myth, the pulls of the dominant culture are sufficient to bring about the integration of large numbers of people from these subcultures into the mainstream of Canadian society. Because the recent immigration into Canada is a larger proportion of society than in the United States, accents unfamiliar to the English ear are more apparent, but the pattern in Canada appears to be similar to that in the United States.

Both societies have major groups that have not been integrated. In Canada, it is the French-speaking popula-

Reprinted with the permission of the author, from *Toronto Daily Star,* August, 20, 1970.

tion of Quebec; in the United States, it is the brownskinned Negroes of the southern rural areas and the large northern cities. The problems of finding the appropriate relationship of these groups to the larger society are quite different, so the parallel phrasing of the problem should not be allowed to mislead us.

In Canada, the Quebeckers have a language, a culture, a territory and a government. Although they have made many modifications of French culture, their origins did represent the transplanting of an established and homogeneous culture from Europe to North America. Insofar as English and French Canada are concerned, the mosaic pattern is profoundly true and is not threatened.

Negroes in the United States, on the other hand, are dispersed. Although one does not wish to deny the existence of some elements of a subculture, even in part perhaps derived from African origins — as in music — the subculture does not lay claim to a language which is so crucial to the Quebec case. Neither did the origins of the Negro people in North America represent the transplanting of an established and homogeneous culture, for American Negroes were brought from various cultures in West Africa, and their native cultures were essentially obliterated by slavery.

There is another respect in which the two societies have different characteristics. The difference is so immense that the problem of national identity is unknown in the United States. Americans know who they are. Even the radical critiques of American society have largely been cast in terms of the failure of that society to fulfil its own aspirations and ideals. In Canada, the situation is quite different.

Identity problem

There are many points of view in Canada on the national identity problem, but there is a virtual unanimity among those who have thought of it that there is a problem. Canadians range from those who deny that there is any need for an explication of the national identity to those who argue for the uniqueness of Canada and who find a radical tradition in Canada that differentiates it clearly from the United States. Some Canadians argue that there is no difference between the two North American cultures. Others see a difference and feel inferior because of it, while still others develop feelings of superiority because of the differences they see. In any case, there is an uncertainty in Canada about the national identity, a factor wholly lacking in the United States.

Although there are similarities between some of the institutions in the two countries, the differences are more striking. On the whole, the differences are greater in the public sphere than in the private, but even the private institutions contain many differences.

Apart from the well-known differences between the parliamentary and congressional systems, there are many differences in the way in which public institutions are organized below the governmental structure. Police, education, and welfare are some examples. Canada's federal police organization, the Royal Canadian Mounted Police, is famous for always getting its man. Not only does this organization perform federal police functions but it also serves as the provincial police in several provinces. The United States simply has no equivalent uniformed national police force.

Both countries have both private and public educational systems, but Canada supports its separate schools with powers of direct taxation. In the

United States, on the other hand, the doctrine of separation of church and state precludes the levying of taxes by private educational authorities. In Canada, higher education has moved almost exclusively into the hands of the public, whereas the United States has continued to preserve the private character of many of its colleges and universities.

In the area of welfare, both countries can be characterized as modern welfare states, although not as complete as some other systems such as Sweden, but here, too, there are differences. Canada has a subsidy for children in its Family Allowance Scheme and it has provincial medical care schemes that are comprehensive. Neither of these institutions can be found in the United States. On the other hand, both countries have unemployment compensation schemes and assistance programs for the needy.

Public institutions

Finally, in the area of public institutions, one must mention the Canadian Broadcasting Corporation, an autonomous public agency with a national network of English-speaking radio and television broadcasting stations and a network of French-speaking stations in Quebec. Although some of its income is derived from private advertising, its public character and mission enables it to develop many programs of excellent quality free from the constraints of the world of commerce. The American National Educational Television scheme is newer and does not compete with the private networks in the same fashion as does the CBC.

Closely related to government are the political parties. Canada has sustained a multiple-party system, whereas the United States, largely because of the presidency, has remained a two-party system. No socialist party has gained power in the United States, but Canada has a provincial socialist government. Part of the rail and air transportation systems in Canada are under public ownership, whereas those in the United States are in private hands supported by public subsidies.

American capital

Canada's will to develop, however, has led to the introduction of American capital in a form which is having a profound impact on the Canadian economic system. Nothing similar exists in the United States. American firms are given, through tax and tariff legislation, inducements to invest in mining and manufacturing enterprises in Canada. This leads to the setting up of plants in Canada which are under the control of the home office in the United States. The duplication of manufacturing in the smaller market of Canada leads to inefficiencies because Canada cannot take advantage of the economies of scale. Research and development resides in the home base of the enterprise, which means that Canadian universities train people who have to work in the United States.

This developing situation has also produced labor unions that operate internationally, but with leadership largely in the hands of Americans in the United States. Contract negotiations in the automobile industry, for example, occur in Detroit, but they affect workers in Oshawa.

To some extent a similar phenomenon is occurring in the cultural sector. Although Canada does have its own media — newspapers, radio and television, magazines — American media penetrate deeply into Canadian cultural life. Much of the content of even the CBC is material that Americans see on the television screens.

The impact of these phenomena is little understood. There are a variety of explanations and reactions to them, both pro-Canadian and anti-American as well as pro-American. There is little doubt, however, that many Canadians fear the implications. Many fear that Canada will lose that which is distinctive and will become, for all practical purposes, the same as the United States.

The question of what is happening to Canada because of these new influences is a profound one. Before trying to answer it, however, the observer needs to determine whether the many differences that have been outlined above have culminated in any essential difference between Americans and Canadians. He will also want to understand why.

CANADA AND U.S. (3)
Society demands less here

Howard Lentner

There is an essential difference between Canada and the United States that is revealed in many different ways. It is a difference in the relationship of the individual to society. In the United States, society makes greater demands on the individual, and the individual responds by giving more of himself to his social groups. In Canada, on the other hand, society demands less of the individual, and he, in turn, gives less of himself.

Aside from certain exceptions, this is the characteristic difference between Americans and Canadians. Our problem now is to understand why this should be so.

The answer lies in the formation and the history of the two peoples. Out of two complexes of experiences, the two peoples have formed two different societies, each with its own strengths and weaknesses; each valid, unique and (to this writer, at least) admirable.

But there is a central explanation which was mentioned earlier in this paper series. It relates to the different ways in which the two peoples have dealt with the ancient political problem of bringing liberty and order together. In their origins, Canadians developed a resolution of the tension between liberty and order. They constructed a government which could govern, and they, although valuing liberty, did not develop the watchword that "eternal vigilance is the price of liberty." In one sense, they trusted each other. Without tension, they could accede to more deferential patterns of life pursued at a

Reprinted with the permission of the author, from *Toronto Daily Star,* August 21, 1970.

more leisurely pace. They have not developed great mythologies or great heroes, for they needed none in the kind of society which they created.

Constant tension

Americans, in their origins, developed a system which maintains a tension between liberty and order. The tension pervades all relationships. One expects much of his government and others, but he also always distrusts their power. This constant tension has led to great change, but it has required great myths and large heroes and grand dreams in order to convince those who distrust. Out of this tension has been borne the greatness of the United States, but the tension has also produced the extremism of America. It has led to cycles of increased tension and release of that tension. In the long run, the United States has held steady to the grand ideals of its Declaration of Independence. Much more is expected of Americans by other Americans, and Americans respond to these expectations.

In public life, there is an intensity of debate in the United States that one seldom sees in Canada. This intensity leads to emotionalism and extremism in debate that force a leader into adopting a stance expected of him by his supporters. This leads to a rhetoric of cliché and to a polarization of conflict. It makes it more difficult to develop reasonable discourse on public issues. The debate in the United States about the war in Viet Nam is perhaps the most dramatic recent example of this phenomenon, but it has occurred many times before.

There are occasions — in the fall of 1968 with respect to the Nigerian civil war, for example — when something approaching the intensity of American debate occurs in Canada. Still, the same degree of intensity is not there, and the expectations of followers and the response of leaders does not lead to the extremism that characterizes American debates.

It is commonplace to observe that the pace of life in Canada is slower and less hectic than in the United States, but it is not commonplace to argue that this is another index of the difference in the relationship of the individual to society.

Approach to work

This pace-of-life phenomenon extends to work. Although some of the differential in productivity can be attributed to capital equipment, different scales of production and so forth, there is also a difference in the approach to work by Americans and Canadians.

Twenty-four-hour gasoline stations are a rare phenomenon in Canada, although evening shopping is not. Marketing techniques are not so efficient in Canada as they are in the United States.

Marketing efficiency relies partly upon mass production. This may account in part for the greater conformity in dress in the United States. But Americans and Canadians also have different attitudes toward dress which conform to the thesis of this paper. When one attends a party in the United States and is dressed differently from most of the guests, he feels embarrassed and is usually invited by his host to remove his jacket and tie or, in another case, to borrow a jacket and tie from his host in order that he should conform with the social group. In contrast, a similar situation in Canada would not be the subject of comment or embarrassment.

The absence of conscription in Canada is another example of the lower level of demand that society puts on the individual.

There are two major exceptions: hockey and the radicals. Canadian hockey fans (and few Canadians do not belong to this group) expect a great deal of their players, and there are few sports or other activities into which individuals throw themselves with such gusto, energy and will. Radical activity is by nature demanding, and radicals by definition are intense. Although very much a minority Canadian radicals do demand much of themselves and of other Canadians.

Canadians are worried about the impact of American cultural and economic influence in their country. This is a recent worry. They have long been troubled by the lack of a national identity. Combining the old and the new, Canadians seek to defend themselves from the colossus of the south by finding the answer to the old problem as a means to preserve what is uniquely Canadian against that which is different. In short, Canadians want to remain independent, with control over their own lives.

Perhaps it would be useful to try to sort out what is vulnerable and what is not.

The origins of Canada cannot be denied. The interpretation and consciousness of those origins can make a difference. Schools in Canada can certainly do more to pass on a consciousness of the Canadian past. Perhaps such an undertaking could be reinforced by popular culture, but the schools are an instrument of the people that is very powerful if used to pass on a culture. To create strong myths and to adulate large heroes, however, is perhaps to undermine what is different about Canada as contrasted with the United States.

Stress biculturalism

The schools could do something else in this regard: they could make Canadian children aware of the bilingual and bicultural nature of their society. A simple but effective beginning would be to have schoolchildren recite their pledge of allegiance and sing O Canada in both English and French. Although much more could be done, this simple exercise would go far in developing an awareness in Canadians of each other.

If bilingualism were to become common in Canada, that alone would be a major defence against the United States. This would involve Canadians expecting much of themselves and their compatriots, but it would set Canadians apart from Americans.

There is no reason to expect that public institutions in Canada are vulnerable to American domination, but the vulnerability of private institutions is quite a different problem. American corporations and some voluntary associations, such as labor unions, already have a major impact in Canada.

For Canadians, it is important to distinguish between control by Americans and the adoption of patterns and forms of organization that are like American patterns. For example, in some cases, the best means to protect independence might be to adopt American research and development and distribution methods in sectors of the Canadian economy. Policies which encourage Canadian entrepreneurs to innovate and compete in the area of organizational technology might be adopted.

Using discretion

This leads to the question of whether one can separate those things which are useful to Canada without adopting those characteristics which Canadians do not want.

Canadians would not choose the growth of conformity and a spreading of intensity which could lead to Americanization in its worst forms of extremism and distrust. That is not a choice that they have to make, however. The useful distinction is between the public and private sectors of life.

Not distrusting government to the same extent that Americans do, Canadians could, without changing themselves profoundly, bring those industries which require a monopoly position under public control. Canada has already nationalized part of its rail and air transportation systems and some of its public utilities, and it already has the CBC in the communications field. Nationalization of other public utilities — such as telephones — would seem to be another step in the appropriate direction.

Because the public sector of Canadian life is the foundation of Canada's uniqueness, enlarging its scope is a way of preserving that uniqueness and a way of insulating a major part of Canada from the influences of the Americanization process. The intensity of effort that would be needed to strengthen the private sector would not, then, spill over into the public life of the country.

American investment will continue. From the Canadian viewpoint, it brings wealth, and few Canadians wish to give that up. But Americans, with all their influence, are marginal to the problem of preserving Canadian life and culture, and Canadians alone must save their own souls. There is little doubt in my mind that they have the capacity to do it and that it is worth the effort.

THE NEW ANTI-AMERICANISM

Robert Fulford

Robert Fulford is the editor of Saturday Night *magazine. He has an extensive background in journalism and broadcasting.*

I classify the two kinds of anti-Americanism I know best as the Old and the New. The Old is the one I grew up with, the one that dominated much of Canada's intellectual life in the 1940s and the 1950s. The New is the one you can see coming over the horizon just about now. It would be

difficult at this point to guess which will finally prove to be the more crippling to the Canadian spirit.

The Old anti-Americanism was based on the simple propostion that England was good and the United States bad. England was cultured and the United States uncultured. Canada, being an extension of England, was therefore better than the United States (though not so good as England). Therefore Canadians could look down on Americans. This was useful,

Reprinted with permission of *Saturday Night,* March 1970.

because we needed someone to look down on.

This form of anti-Americanism ran into trouble when we discovered that (1) Europe, especially England, was becoming Americanized and apparently loving it; (2) We Canadians were far more North American than European, and there was nothing much we could do about it.

Before it died, the Old anti-Americanism helped to poison certain aspects of our culture. At best it clearly limited our comprehension of the dynamic, attractive, appalling nation on whose doorstep we were living; it kept us from looking, as seriously as we should have, at the best of American culture, while at the same time we were swamped by the worst. This attitude particularly infested the education system, which assumed an attitude of superiority so far out of relation to the facts that it now seems all but incredible. At school I had it explained to me so often that the education I was getting was superior to the American kind that, when I finally met Americans, I was astonished that they could read and write.

We all said farewell to this attitude sometime in the middle of 1960s. But very late in the 1960s another, similar frame of mind began to form itself:

The New anti-Americanism is different, in several ways, but it's probably no more useful as the basis for a culture. The New anti-Americanism begins with the proposition that the United States is a colossal empire and a corrupt one, and that its imperial designs are forcing its corrupt nature on us, crushing the Canadian Spirit. The United States, therefore, in producing books we can read or paintings we can look at, and teachers to work in our universities, is not only doing us a grave disservice but is probably

carrying out some diabolical scheme that challenges our very existence.

Not everything that results from this viewpoint is necessarily bad. Some people require that, before, they can be *for* something (Canada, in this case) they must first be against something else (the United States, in this case). Not everyone can love his own country and what it creates simply because it is his own and is related to him. For people who can't manage this, a certain anti-Americanism may encourage the creation of patriotism.

But quite early in its career, the New anti-Americanism reached a remarkable level of hysteria. The controversy centred on the Governor-General's Awards, given each year for the best Canadian books. One of the three judges for the 1969 English-language awards was Warren Tallman, a professor of English at the University of British Columbia. Tallman has lived in Vancouver fourteen years, has written about Canadian literature often, and has earned the respect of an entire generation of West Coast poets. But there's one thing wrong with him. He's only a landed immigrant, not a Canadian. He's still a citizen of the United States.

Therefore, Robin Mathews—who is certainly, by now, our most celebrated anti-American professor, and the noisiest proponent of the New anti-Americanism — organized a compaign against Tallman. In April, in a widely circulated letter, Mathews attacked Tallman as a U.S. imperialist ("conscious or unconscious"), attacked the Canada Council for allowing Tallman to help choose the Governor-General's Awards, and invited Tallman to resign. Mathews' wife and five Carleton University students picketed the Canada Council offices, handing out leaflets calling for Tallman's resignation.

The protest was in all ways unreasonable. Mathews might be justified, perhaps, if he suggested that an American, visiting the country for a month or an academic year, would be an improper judge of our literature. But Tallman knows the country, knows our literature, and has committed a good part of his life to Canada. Moreover, the tradition in Canadian literature, as Mathews should know, leans towards the habit of adopting whoever cares to adopt us. Brian Moore and Malcolm Lowry are "Canadian" writers, according to various Canadian books, though both were immigrants and neither chose to spend his whole life here.

The argument of Mathews and his supporters is based on the narrowest sort of nationalism. I've been troubled, since the universities controversy arose last year, by the fact that people objecting to American professors in Canadian universities have failed to make the distinction between Americans who just stop here in mid-career and those who make a more or less permanent contribution to the country. Mathews is the co-editor of the most substantial contribution to the debate, *The Struggle for Canadian Universities* (New Press, Toronto, 1969), and his recent action tends to discredit further the whole dubious collection of views with which he is associated.

THE MENACE IS THE MESSAGE

Pauline Jewett

Pauline Jewett was a Liberal member of Parliament and is now Director of the Institute of Canadian Studies at Carleton University in Ottawa.

I cannot, of course, speak for all political circles, but I do recall very well the use of the word "retaliation" on many occasions, within my own party and in Parliament, while I was a Liberal MP. It was used chiefly in the context of Canadian-American relations when the fear was expressed that the U.S. would "retaliate" against Canada, through some specific act or policy (quite legal), should Canada pursue a certain course of action.

I could give several concrete examples of this but the most vivid in my memory concerns the magazine legislation of 1964 which excluded Canadian advertisements in American journals from tax exemption and so gave Canadian journals protection. The Liberal caucus was generally in favour of this legislation and also in favour of having it include *Time* and *Reader's Digest*. There was only one individual strongly opposed to the latter and he had *Reader's Digest* — a large employer — in his riding! The cabinet, I gather, was a bit more split, being closer no doubt to political reality. The "political reality" in this instance was, quite simply, fear of

Reprinted with permission of Pauline Jewett, Director, Institute of Canadian Studies, Carleton University, contributor to *An Independent Foreign Policy for Canada?* edited by Stephen Clarkson.

American retaliation. Members of caucus had it explained to them by members of cabinet that, should the government go ahead and include *Time* and *Reader's Digest,* Washington (in response, no doubt, to domestic pressures) would "retaliate" against us. A tentative agreement on some particular matter (automobiles perhaps?) would not go through. Or the President would cease supporting us vis-à-vis Congress with respect to some proposed Congressional act.

Maybe we politicians are just naïve. After all, we are not in the State Department or External where people "know" that these things are not going to happen. But I can only say that the fear was there and that past experience had shown that it was justified. Professor Safarian notes that there have been few occasions when we suffered the act of retaliation. But there have been a sufficient number of times when we feared its possibility that the threat of retaliation has conditioned governmental attitudes into general timidity.

What concerns one most about all this is the mesmerizing effect it has on Canadian policy-makers. Instead of doing things that they think are desirable or that the Canadian public may want done, our policy-makers do things that the American public or the American government or powerful American pressure-groups want. Not always, of course. Not on bread-and-butter issues like selling wheat to China. But on broader matter of foreign policy like *recognizing* China or the war in Vietnam, our governments waffle. They do not take the positions that either their own judgment or, in many instances, Canadian public opinion demands.

Canadian politicians frequently *do* have views substantially different from those of their American counterparts. I could not help noticing this when I was a member of the Canada-U.S. Interparliamentary Group. The Canadian MPs and the Senators taking part in the discussions found themselves — regardless of party — in substantial agreement on a number of subjects — the cold war, China, Nato, Cuba, and so on — and in substantial disagreement with the American Congressmen and Senators taking part, Democrats and Republicans (barring Wayne Morse). Both sides noticed this difference in attitudes. Similarly, Canadian public opinion is frequently at odds with American. One can look at the polls, for example, on China or, more recently, on Vietnam, and compare. Or one can look at the different attitudes taken by the churches in the two countries on these and other matters.

I despair of our ever transcending our caution. We *do* have a different view about a variety of matters but because of our fears (and our chief fear nowadays is the fear of American retaliation), we rarely take positions reflecting our own judgment or responding to public opinion in our own country. Our caution does a great disservice not only to ourselves internally but, most serious of all, to an independent, creative contribution to world problems.

SPEAK AMERICAN OR SPEAK ENGLISH: A CHOICE OF IMPERIALISMS

Doug Fetherling

Doug Fetherling is a Toronto author and poet and a frequent contributor to Saturday Night, *the* Globe and Mail *the* Toronto Star, *and to CBC radio and television. His books of poems include* Our Man in Utopia.

The day I quit my last American newspaper job to move to Toronto, my fellow city room workers glanced up from their Underwoods, laid aside their Lucky Strikes and one by one doled out the routine good-bye handshakes. Or at least all of them except our ancient editor emeritus — a 1920s Montreal *Herald* writer and a self-ordained veteran of "fifty peripatetic years in this racket." He waited his turn, dragged me behind a fake Doric column, and offered a bit of farewell advice. "Remember, son," he said, "those Canadians spell funny."

I doubt that hoary member of the old school knew the full wisdom of his words. He, having risen from copy boy to top editor in a scant half-century, merely meant to tell me that he'd been around and had seen a few older British spellings set down by some northern hand. It was a subtle, old-fashioned statement of his experience, like the way he wore his hat in the office. Doubtless his English opposite number would have warned me of ugly Americanisms which have crept into the Queen's English in the great Dominion across the sea. Both, of course, would be correct in saying English Canadians write (and speak) funny. But right for the wrong reasons. For the Canadian language, if it can be called that, is a mishmash affair wrought from a hopeless shambles and quickly rising to a crescendo of confusion.

In linguistics and rhetoric, as in most things, English Canadians are presumed by Americans to be rather British and are presumed by the British to be rather American. When it comes to language, most Canadians don't know where they stand or why. Beleaguered Canadian wavers of the Union Jack who employ *tely* and *motorcar* one day can be mistaken for Californians the next. Nationalists who lash out against Yankee imperialism while forgetting the lyrics of *God Save the Queen* may do so in a tongue only partly logical to either enemy, or to themselves. In extremes, being an English-speaking Canadian is akin to being a Belgian banker who, linguistic-

Reprinted with permission of Doug Fetherling, *Saturday Night,* September 1970.

ally speaking, goes where the weather suits his clothes.

I'm not suggesting we immediately concoct something on the order of Esperanto. I merely contend most Anglo-Canadians, even those who communicate for a living, know little, really, about these two biggest non-native influences on the language.

Broadly, neither is a bad influence. The Americans are of course better innovators of language. This is illustrated nowhere better than in the terminologies needed each time some new technological force arrives. Ignoring the current Space Age (which, insofar as English speakers go, is dominated by the Americans), look at that previous great leap forward, the automobile, which developed on both continents at about the same time. Lacking names for the front and rear cavities of the auto, the Americans lighted upon *hood* and *trunk*. The English took the terms *bonnet* and *boot*, which were previously in vehicular existence with regards to the stage coach. Going back still further, think of the invention of the steam locomotive. The newly-thought-of triangular metal device on the front of the engine that scooted obstacles off the tracks had to be called something. The Americans called it a *cowcatcher* while the British, in a typical outpouring of creativity, named it a *plough*.

Conversely, the British influence upon English Canadian language has the benefit of being stabler, more time-proven, not to mention being more valuable in terms of Canadian heritage and more interchangeable with the English spoken in parts of the world outside of North America and the U.K.

In a recent magazine column an Ontario Conservative leader stated he was "old-fashioned" because he still put a *u* in *colour*. The idea is absurd.

What is called Canadian usage — the collage embodying *u's* in words like *colour,* the un-American spellings of *centre* and *theatre,* the U.S. double quotes around single quotes, et cetera — is what has been taught in schools in all the provinces for some time. In fact, a Canadian book publisher once had to reprint some 30,000 elementary textbooks for a British Columbia school system after it was discovered American alternatives had slipped into print. True, the American ways are increasingly coming into favour with Canadians, ostensibly because of American media pollution. American immigrants, I think, rather enjoy these, for them, "quaint" bits of usage upon arrival here, and as individuals do little to drive them under. And those who do not adhere are counterbalanced by the nearly one million British immigrants who have settled in Canada in the past twenty years. The discrepancies are greater and the intricacies more intricate than I'm making them sound. And the non-English-speaking immigrant to non-French Canada picks up whatever or whichever he comes in contact with. Pity the poor immigrant.

The media make up the biggest influence on usage, and the great barrage of American magazines and books aimed at Canada is not conducive to an indigenous Canadian anything. Even the home-grown newspapers list southward when it comes to style.

With minor exceptions, the papers follow the guides set down in the style books of the Canadian Press, publications which are patterned more on their U.S. counterparts' (Associated Press, United Press International) than on those of British or other wire services. Although the CP manuals instruct their users to "avoid Americanisms and the writing style of *Time,*" they have forsaken the longer British spellings of many words and stress *labor, behavior, neighbor* and the like. But at the same time they approve only the longer *cheque* and *cigarette* (the latter, perhaps, in deference to tobacco advertisers, who apparently think it more elegant).

In words such as *centre*, the CP members concede the original British spellings are in popular usage in Canada and are therefore correct for their purpose. But they have become current, at least in part, because Canadian eyes naturally retain what they see in newspapers year after year. The papers in themselves possess the subtle power to revamp the Canadian language over a long period of time, just as they have already enlarged (and nearly wrecked) it over the years. "Splashdown probe slated to kickoff factfinding mission" and similar sentences have little basis in the accepted history of the English language and are products of the deprived minds of men born after 1900.

In modern newspapers the tendency is make everything as short as possible, there being only so much space into which accounts of wars, rapes and disasters can be crammed. Also, the modern media frown upon individual writing styles, preferring instead to have everything as nearly interchangeable as possible. (This is why our newspapers are so boring compared with those of the nineteenth century.) Aside from minor impositions, Canadian editors are forced to use CP style in papers because substantially altering syntax and spelling in teletype copy would involve casting aside the accompanying computer tape and manually setting type for revised versions in their own shops — a costly and time-consuming task. And such Canadian mass magazines as there are often are edited by former newspapermen who

got out when they could and whose old habits die hard.

In the non-print media Canada fares slightly better. Both the CBC and the National Film Board were originally set up under Mackenzie King by native and British labour, who favoured quaint "Canadianisms." To this day (and to its credit) the CBC prefers hiring local announcers to give regional broadcasts that special flair. But in at least a couple of cases this has backfired when the airwaves were filled with dialects which, because of dramatic shifts in the "accepted spoken standard," no longer existed outside the corporation's studios. But the CBC remains the best mirror of what is good Canadian English. W. A. Brodie, long the CBC's head of broadcast language and now serving in an advisory capacity, conducts a fortnightly column for announcers and other personnel in the CBC's house organ, *Closed Circuit*. There, he constantly warns against Americanisms, points out common errors, and generally waxes intelligent. For all its good, however, the CBC's word is not that of God. I'm certain that officially retaining the British pronunciations of *lieutenant* (leftenant) and *schedule* (rather than the American schedule) has confused as many Canadians as the CBC has listeners.

In language, as in most things, the quickest way to go completely mad is to follow all the rules to the letter. But since Canada has no Forty Immortals to pronounce what is not, the average Canadian is so confused about what is "his" and what is "theirs" that the Canadian language, spoken and written, has been reduced to a state only slightly stabler than the Canadian economy. The fault does not lie with the average citizen, although the responsibility for straightening out things is his. If Canadian English is to discontinue being a succotash, he must come to terms with it. He must realize that British English is not bad merely because it's British. Saying lift for elevator does not make you a colonial. And while good points and bad inherent in it can be argued back and forth, the English of the educated Briton, all else it is, is fairly consistent.

American English, while also having its merits and drawbacks, is the present-day language of imperialism, just as British English was in the past century. It's not by chance that the Japanese word for cigarette lighter has become *zippo*. The Americans don't want Canada's people, they want Canada's future; and they don't want a language, they want a code. One grunt means "fill 'er up," two grunts mean "gimme a Coke."

It takes two in order to tango. Know what is American, what is British, what is Canadian. Don't become a walking Maclean-Hunter style book, which cautions that *witness stand* is American but *witness box* is Canadian. Watch those late, late movies depicting the Old Bailey and find out where it really came from. Then, keeping an ear open to what your neighbours use, make your own decision. Perhaps what is necessary is appraisal instead of acquiescence.

Part 2

Long ere the second centennial arrive, there will be some forty to fifty great States, among them Canada and Cuba. . . . The Pacific will be ours, and the Atlantic mainly ours. There will be daily electric communication with every part of the globe. What an age! What a land! Where, elsewhere, one so great? The individuality of one nation must then, as always, lead the world. Can there be any doubt who the leader ought to be?

Walt Whitman

Are our economic relationships with United States making Walt Whitman's prophecy come true? In what ways and how strongly is our economy tied to the American economy?

A CONTINENTAL EMBRACE

Like so many things that are decided in America, the strike that started this week at General Motors can be another little reminder to Canadians of the incompleteness of their power of decision in their affairs. A negotiation between an American management and a substantially American trade union fails in Detroit and, along with some 350,000 employees of General Motors in the United States, 20,000 or so are on strike in Canada. Nobody has anything to complain of. It has all been done in a proper manner. The Canadian motor workers were not against striking; a majority of them anticipated Tuesday's strike order by staying out on Monday.

The motor vehicles and parts industry in Canada is 95 per cent under American control. Canada's economy benefits substantially from the American management's decisions that place subsidiary plants across the Great Lakes in Ontario and Canadian government policy has encouraged the development, as well it might, since the practical alternative would have been to be without a viable motor industry at all.

It remains a worry that decisions affecting Canadian life are being taken outside Canada and not by Canadians. Canada's labour movement, dominated as it is by the big "international" (that is, preponderantly American) unions, shows signs of sharing it. A parliamentary committee in Ottawa, reporting this summer on Canadian-American relations, brooded over this problem of putting a Canadian stamp on the affairs of the international unions in Canada. It proposed "guidelines" under which each international union would organise its Canadian locals into a Canadian section which, said the committee, ought to have "complete authority" in collective bargaining, the settlement of disputes and the conclusion of collective agreements, "which should not require approval in the United States." But the unions, having taken the trouble to follow the big American concerns into Canada, will not readily acquiesce in having their bargaining power carved up.

As is natural, most matters affecting Canadian-American relations get a lot more attention in Canada than in the United States. To complaints of American dominance of Canadian industry, officials in Washington reply that it is not American policy to bring any such dominance about, and never has been. The same cannot be said, they add, of Canadian policy. A long period of protective Canadian tariffs combined with imperial preferences influenced American manufacturers to get behind the tariff barrier by establishing small subsidiaries to serve the Canadian market. The modern development, which has caused foreign investment in Canada to grow since 1945 faster even than the gross national product, is the outcome of

Reprinted with permission of *The Economist*, September 19, 1970.

different forces: the country's insatiable need for development capital, the preference of Canadian investors for American over Canadian stocks for their own private portfolios, and the relative drying up of British and other foreign sources of new industrial capital. Between 1948 and 1968, some 85 per cent of Canada's new foreign capital came from the United States.

The Canadian government's series of development programmes has fostered the growth of foreign-owned firms, as the report of the parliamentary external affairs committee points out. In its efforts to develop advanced branches of industry and backward regions of the country, Ottawa paid out $358 million in grants and subsidies to selected industries in the four fiscal years ended in 1969: foreign-owned firms got $180 million of this. This is Canadian policy, not American. The economic results have even been good. Conceding that a problem does, nevertheless, exist, the American official will observe that it is not an economic problem but a psychological one.

Like the Parliament in Ottawa, the Trudeau government has been showing concern with the problems, psychological or not, that can arise when a country has an unusually large slice of its economy owned or controlled from abroad. A government task force with Professor Melville Watkins as its chairman reported in 1968 that the extent of foreign control of Canadian industry was "unique among the industrialised nations." Most of it was American. Out of an accumulated volume of $15.9 billion of foreign direct investment in Canada in 1963, 80 per cent came from the United States, 12 per cent from Britain; without doubt the American share is bigger now. In the manufacturing and extractive industries it amounts to a preponderance.

The Watkins report listed the sources of tension inherent in this situation. Most of them would not count for so much if the foreign interest would present itself as a local concern, with a substantial local shareholding and some independent Canadian directors not looking to Denver or Pittsburgh or New York for approval or promotion. But the wholly owned subsidiary suits the average big American concern better; it wants full control. Here is one "source of tension."

Granted this, the parent company is not disposed to regard its wholly owned subsidiary as a separate entity for accounting purposes: so the Canadian public is not given much information about its affairs and "government departments find themselves deciding important matters of policy without adequate statistics." The subsidiary is liable not to be responsive to Canadian wishes about capital transfers or corporate tax policy. On such matters it is liable to be all too responsive, from the Canadian point of view, to its home government. Canada went through financial scares in 1965 and again in 1968 because of anticipations, exaggerated as it turned out, of the repercussions of the bad American balance of international payments on the financial behaviour of American subsidiaries in Canada.

Canada is always at a disadvantage in trying to get them to follow its, and not American, policy in anti-trust matters (where the Canadian interest may suggest a merger, which some consent agreement between the parent company and the Department of Justice in Washington forbids) or in their decisions to trade or not to trade with communist countries, a matter on which the views of the Canadian and

United States governments have always diverged. This is the kind of question that one of Mr. Trudeau's ministers, Mr. Herb Gray, is grappling with just now, since he has been entrusted with the preparation of draft proposals for the cabinet. There will have to be legislation; public opinion has become emphatic and a failure to do something to assert that foreign-owned companies belong to the Canadian economy and are subject to Canadian law is something that the Trudeau government can afford less than any other.

On either side the men who conduct relations between governments exert themselves to keep tempers down and contentious things in perspective. Thus, while there is a downright clash of wills about the limits of Canadian sovereignty in the straits of the Arctic archipelago, American officials deny that there is any suspicion on their minds that any Canadian authority might actually interfere with an American ship, even far away up there. The question is one of principle, they explain: the United States resists national claims to control of international straits in other places: how can it concede to Canada what it would deny to Indonesia?

Still, American interests press untiringly on a Canada rich in resources, poor in capital, and not so well off in the higher industrial and entrepreneurial skills. They hanker after "continental" policies for oil and gas (to which Canadians reply that they are prepared to discuss trade but not plans for the allocation of their resources). Now and then the broader, to Canadians more menacing, term "a continental energy policy" finds expression, as it did through Mr. Nixon's Secretary of the Interior, Mr. Walter Hickel, in May when Mr. Hickel mentioned not only oil and gas but water, coal and atomic energy (that is, Canadian uranium) in one breath.

Mr. Joe Greene, the Canadian Minister of Energy, Mines and Resources, replied quickly that such an all-embracing common policy would amount to "an abnegation of sovereignty" for Canada. As for water, he said: "Canada has no water for sale." Even the Canadians most friendly to the United States and most deprecating about the new wave of Canadian nationalism turn hard when water is mentioned. The United States, they are convinced, would rather help itself to Canada's water than go to the trouble and expense of making better use of its own: a belief not without substance, but which authorities in Washington deny with some heat. An underlying conflict exists between American desires for a "rational" exploitation of the resources of the North American continent and the Canadian desire to be, or to become, distinct. "I am afraid of anything that leads to a rational organisation of North America," one Canadian put it. Evidently an argument has begun that will not end for a long time.

THE COLD WAR IN RESOURCES

Fred Knelman

Fred Knelman is chairman of the Department of Humanities of Science at Sir George Williams University in Montreal.

With only six and a half percent of the world's population, the United States consumes about 50 percent of all the world's energy and resources. This means that each person — man, woman and child — in the United States on the average consumes eight times as much energy and resources as each person in the entire rest of the world.

The United States has some 50 percent of the world's telephones, over 60 percent of the world's electric refrigerators, 70 percent of the television sets and 90 percent of the world's computers. There are almost 100 million automobiles in the United States, annual production now running at over 10 million. Americans consume 25 percent of all the beer in the world. By 1985 there could be as many as 275 million people in the United States, and by the year 2000 the population could approach some 350 million. Canada is expected to have a population of 38 million in 2000.

But even more than its present voracious consumption of fuel, power, minerals, metals, chemicals, plastics, etc., the United States is dedicated to an incredible growth in its use of all critical materials. The average doubling period for the consumption of energy and key resources in the United States is less than one generation.

There is another vital resource the US is using far more than its share of — the air we breathe. American industries are consuming an enormous amount of the world's oxygen.

Thus, early in 1980 it is estimated that the United States will consume over 80 percent of the world's energy and major resources. Projections for the year 2000 are even more fantastic. The Gross National Product (GNP) will soar from just under $1 trillion in 1970 to over $3 trillion. Automobile production will reach 26 million and there will be 244 million cars on the roads of America. The statistics of death by accident and emission will rise proportionately. Steel production will triple or quadruple and electric power is expected to go up by a factor of five.

In the past the United States has used enough raw materials to account for half of the total world's steel output, more than half of the world's oil and 90 percent of its natural gas. But the growth rates now anticipated will increase these proportions in the future. Should the rest of the world achieve American levels of consump-

Reprinted with permission of F. H. Knelman, "The Cold War in Resources," *Weekend Magazine*, June 27, 1970.

tion, over a hundred-fold increase of the world's energy and resources would be required.

Yet, from a resource viewpoint, the United States is a have-not nation. Some 33 separate minerals and other basic materials are on a "critical" list. Among those the United States must now import and continue to do so on an accelerating scale are crude oil (30 percent imported), iron ore (40 percent), bauxite (95 percent), copper (75 percent), lead (50 percent), zinc (55 percent), potash (over 50 percent), uranium (over 50 percent), pulpwood, timber, chromite (95 percent), manganese (95 percent), rubber (95 percent) and gold 90 (percent).

What do all these figures mean? Actually, the arithmetic of resources is simple to understand. The United States cannot grow at its present or intended rate without vastly increased dependence upon foreign resources and energy. When we take into account that the entire developed world and, in particular, the USSR and China, are equally dedicated to this kind of growth, then the conclusion is simple. There is no way to share the world resource pie. The pie itself is not large enough.

History has witnessed the rise and decline of supreme world powers from ancient Greece to Britain of the 19th century. Each in its time was a major consumer and producer. But nothing in the past compares to the world's localized affluence in the United States today.

What was once obtained by war and piracy, a technique not entirely abandoned, is now obtained by blackmail, barter or investment. There is truly an imperialist principle in resource exploitation, a resource drain to the United States, a resource glut-

ton which consumes and is planning to consume the great proportion of the world's energy and nonrenewable resources. It is inevitable that Canada, resource-rich but population-poor, by virtue of its proximity to the resource-hungry but rich United States, will be the target of enormous pressures. United States corporations already control, among others, our petroleum, natural gas, paper, potash, nickel and copper.

It is well to understand the nature and point of attack of these pressures, as well as the principles and human values involved. Will we simply sell these "quick assets" irresponsibly or secure by hard bargaining the highest price short of extortion? Will we thus be reduced to a limited level of industrial development by this impoverishment of resources or restriction on manufacturing? If we resist will it be for venal patriotism, national resentment or clear principles?

The Hudson Institute, Herman Kahn's expensive think-tank for thinking the unthinkable, while soft-selling a predicted future that is inevitable, has indicated that Canada's position in the developed world will slip from fourth to seventh by 1980, exceeded in GNP per capita by France, West Germany, Japan, Sweden and Switzerland.

The issue of foreign ownership involves basic principles of national identity, purpose and development. There is a clear and present danger that we might be selling our industrial potential for a mess of pottage (potash in Saskatchewan). The pressure points can be identified with those specific resources we have and the United States wants — uranium, zinc, lead, iron ore, gold, copper, nickel, mercury, potash, petroleum, natural gas, paper and water. Many of these resources already constitute major Canadian exports to the United States. Many of them are already controlled by United States corporations. Water, like the beaver, remains a unique symbol of Canadian identity, and in the end much of the wheeling and dealing in President Nixon's "continental energy plan" will involve water.

The United States now uses 400 billion gallons per year, and this will become 900 billion by 1990. Present and future rates of all types of pollution, including thermal, make water the world's most critical resource. Canada has one-fourth of the world's fresh water and the largest coastline in the world. By 1990 we will have some 770 billion gallons (two-thirds from British Columbia) available for export. But a special committee appointed by former president Lyndon Johnson stated that all fresh water in the United States will be polluted by the 1980s.

This world resource analysis allows us to indulge in the dubious act of predicting the future. In a large sense the United States already lives in the future, and using that country as a model provides insights into the way the entire world is moving. It is the United States which has come nearest to completing what has come to be designated as the technological order, the supremacy and sovereignty of an accumulation of technical means and techniques acting largely as a closed, self-perpetuating system outside nature and man's will.

The United States is the first scientific-industrial or technological society (what Herman Kahn calls "post-industrial") in which technical knowledge is continuously being used for social innovations. This developing world system of the technological order has rewards in terms of the immediacy and size of payoff in power and profit as to prove irresistible. It is

also largely independent of ideology as far as the great powers are concerned, each being committed to the power race.

Given this background, we can now discern the development of a pattern in US-Canada relations in which resources constitute the central issue. Projected United States needs of certain key materials are such that Americans will want unhampered access to some 90 to 95 percent of all these, no matter where they are on this continent or in its continental waters.

Beginning with the bargaining over our British Columbia water resources (General A. G. L. McNaughton was our first resource patriot), a cold war in resources began which will increase in intensity in the next few decades. Within this framework we can easily understand present manoeuvring and manipulating as simple jockeying for position in the resource race. These actions include President Nixon's instructions to his state department to examine with Canada a continental energy plan; Prime Minister Trudeau's move to prevent the sale of Denison Mines Limited to the United States' Continental Oil Company, thus preventing foreign control of 90 percent of Canada's uranium; President Nixon's naked power play in restricting oil imports from Canada "during the period of transition to an alternative United States-Canada energy policy"; the developing issue of coastal sovereignty and Arctic jurisdiction, and Canada's strong stand on policing pollution in Arctic waters; Energy Minister J. J. Greene's warning that a new set of rules of ownership is being developed for the Canadian economy.

All these presage increasing confrontations as a resurgence of Canadian nationalism demands retention of resource ownership. Hopefully, our politicians are sincere and we are not simply bargaining for better prices. In any case we should help them be sincere. What is at stake is the complete ownership and exploitation of Canada by the United States. Our choice will be reduced to becoming the 51st state or to be kept in a permanent position of limited development.

Nixon's statement that a "unique degree of security" can be achieved by energy integration means we will have to accept the United States' definition of security — the Safeguard ABM system, the arms race, the Southeast Asian commitment, NATO and the endless China confrontations. Canada's world mediating role will be forever destroyed with the destruction of her national identity.

There is one consideration to which we must pay heed since it involves our own and the world's survival. If we assist the United States in its blind, uncontrolled growth, we will all perish in either a degraded environment or a world nuclear holocaust. Without controls, both war and a collapsed biosphere become inevitable. We have many allies among Americans who share this same fear. Even some economists point out that if we subtract Gross National Pollution from Gross National Product we are in a period of declining net wealth as well as health.

Pollution rises proportionately to industrial expansion, while the costs of pollution rise at an even higher rate. These costs are now estimated in the United States as $30 billion per year and could rise to $60 billion per year in the 1980s.

The United States now contributes some 40 to 50 percent of the pollutants in the world. It is simple to see what a burden of cost and health the United States places and will continue to place on the world.

Furthermore, the United States, now dependent on the rest of the world for its basic raw materials, is facing mounting pressures for a deepening dependence. This, in turn, intensifies the crises arising from such dependence: foreign ownership and intervention, a struggle for world resources, even a kind of resource war.

Pollution costs, whether by an individual industry or a nation, tend to be externalized or deferred. In effect, this creates a competition to pollute since this allows a greater share of the hidden subsidy or social costs of pollution.

In a somewhat analagous fashion, there is a global imperialist principle in pollution in that a powerful postindustrial society like the United States prefers to seek the importation of key materials from those countries with greater production benefits, including minimum costs for pollution control. This is cheaper than developing costly technological innovations, exploiting low-grade resources or recycling and reclaiming wastes.

This is so despite the claims of the new technocrats or "new cornucopians" with their religious belief in the infallibility of technology to provide answers independent of economic viability or the human condition. The climax of ultimate technology and depletion of resources occurs together. Thus the pattern of United States investment is for capital to flow to resources in less-developed, resource-rich or population-poor countries such as Australia, Canada, Spain, South Africa and South America. This pattern is now well established and, as we have stated, by the 1980s the United States will be importing the major proportion of large-tonnage metals such as iron, copper, lead, aluminum and zinc, thus adding to its present import burden.

Remember — these are nonrenewable resources. There is only one crop, and when it is harvested there is no more. Without conservation, even water and wood are nonrenewable. There are now 20 critical resource materials in the world which will be in short supply or virtually depleted soon after the year 2000.

We live a disposable life of no deposit and no return, a world of large waste for a few and a large want for many. We are blindly compelled by an Everest syndrome in technology. We have made a theology of material progress. There is a universal crisis in human values. If we do not change our values the world will end with either a bang or a whimper.

Before it is too late we should resist the United States commitment to uncontrolled growth, as deadly to biological cells as to nations. We should do this out of principles, not venal patriotism or misdirected resentment. We should support all political moves in and out of Canada that resist the pathology of blind growth. Otherwise we must face the alternatives — joining the US or being relegated to a position of minimal advancement.

WATER:
THE SELLOUT
THAT COULD SPELL
THE END OF CANADA

Walter Stewart

Walter Stewart is an associate editor of Maclean's.

One Monday evening in 1979, Mrs. Jessica Johnson, suburban Winnipeg housewife, steps up to her sinkful of dirty dishes, sighs and turns on the water. The tap gives a tentative gurgle, one liquid drop appears, hangs, quivers and falls to the soiled dishes below. Then nothing. "Damn it to hell," says Mrs. Jessica Johnson, suburban Winnipeg housewife, "the bloody water is shut off again." At the heart of Canada, the richest nation in the world in water resources, there is no way for her to do her dishes; but that same day nine billion gallons of Canadian water cross the U.S. border to serve the farms, factories and cities of the American southwest.

On January 13, 1981, the directors of a manufacturing company meet in Regina to discuss the proposed opening of a new plant on the prairies. It is decided to drop the project,

Reprinted with permission of Walter Stewart in *Maclean's*, November 1970.

because there might not be enough water available to run the plant. The diversion tunnels carrying Canadian water to the U.S. are too far away for ready access; besides, the water is already spoken for — in the U.S.

On September 6, 1983, the President meets with a small group of advisers in the White House to discuss an urgent matter. The coming elections in British Columbia look likely to return a socialist government, which might be hostile to the U.S., might even want to interfere with the massive water-diversion systems on which the western states have come to depend. What should the President do? Opinion is divided. Some advisers feel that any attempt to influence the election will backfire, others that a little discreet lobbying might turn the trick. One aide, quickly shouted down, suggests, "If necessary, we should take the damn army in there, and show the damn Canadians what's what." No decision is reached, but the President closes the meeting on an ominous note. "Anybody who thinks this country will stand idly by while our water is cut off," he says, "has another think coming."

Fantasy?

Certainly.

Preposterous!

Perhaps.

It could never happen!

Oh, no?

Already, water shortages have turned off taps in Metro Toronto (in July 1969); already, the problem of adequate supplies for industry on the prairies is causing concern; already, Canada is drifting toward the export of water to the U.S., with everything that implies for the interlinking of the two countries — and everything that implies is a very great deal indeed.

This is not because there is a government policy to sell our resources to the Americans, but because there is no policy at all on that subject, and no haste to develop one. The federal government has been aware of the issue for more than five years; it was on September 2, 1964, in the House of Commons, that Arthur Laing (then Northern Affairs Minister, now Public Works Minister) described water export as "probably the greatest issue that will confront Canadians in the next several decades."

Apparently the government hasn't felt confronted, though; when I recently asked the Minister of Energy, Mines and Resources, J. J. Greene, whether Canada should or would sell water to the U.S., he replied, "This precise issue hasn't come up . . . There is no policy . . . I haven't the information on which to base a decision."

If the precise issue hasn't come up, it should; if there is no policy, it should be developed; if information is lacking, it should be sought, for in the five years since Laing made his statement the question of water export has moved from the world of dreams to that of practical politics; there is a good chance it will be settled while our government is still telling us there is nothing to discuss.

Everything I have said so far will be denied in Ottawa and Washington, where the official view is that the U.S. has never, formally, asked to buy Canadian water, and we have never, formally, offered to sell it; so why worry? That official view needs to be put into perspective, and to do that I have to do something I don't like to do — break an off-the-record confidence.

Go back to 1964. At that time, an American engineering firm proposed a

$100-billion plan (which I'll describe later) to draw off Canadian water for U.S. use. The plan was called NAWAPA — the North American Water And Power Alliance — and it provoked heated discussion in Canada. Northern Affairs Minister Laing set forth the government view in a tough, pull-no-punches speech at Edmonton on October 24, 1964, in which he declared: "We deny categorically that there is anything like a continental resource in respect of water." The subject seemed closed.

Not long after, I went to call on a cabinet member vitally concerned with water, and he reaffirmed the government stand. However, after I had put away my notebook and was about to leave his office, he said, "You should know, for your own information, that something like NAWAPA is not merely feasible, it's inevitable." When I asked why, then, we seemed to be repudiating it, he bobbed his head sagely and said, "We are establishing a bargaining position, and the best bargaining position is to say 'No.' "

The cabinet minister who made that statement was Arthur Laing.

Are we still establishing a bargaining position? I don't know. J. J. Greene says not, and top officials in his department say that if Canada ever sells water to the U.S. it will be only after we are sure our own needs have been met for the foreseeable future. Just the same, there is no policy either for or against water export, and there are a number of signs that, yes, if the Americans want our water, they can have it:

● In 1964, the Western Water Development Subcommittee of the U.S. Senate came out flatly for the purchase of Canadian water. Senator Frank Moss of Utah, who chaired that committee, told me recently, "I am impressed by activity on your side of the border," and, "It is my opinion the prospects are much improved."

● A vast array of plans, projects, schemes, concepts and proposals aimed at moving our water to the U.S. has blossomed on both sides of the border. None of these has received government approval, but one of them, the Central North American Water Project, is the brainchild of E. Roy Tinney, Acting Director of the Policy and Planning Branch of our Department of Energy. Tinney's proposal was made before he joined the department.

● Water importation has been taken under study by two key U.S. policy groups, the National Water Commission in Washington and the Western States Water Council in Salt Lake City, Utah.

● While there have been no government-to-government talks on water, exchanges at the unofficial level are frequent. For instance, Lewis G. Smith, a Denver engineer with an imaginative proposal for tapping northern water, flew to the Yukon at the request of Commissioner James Smith to explain his concept to the Territorial Council, and Jay Bingham, Executive Director of the Western States Water Council, flew to Ottawa to confer with our experts.

● Last December, Energy Minister Greene met with U.S. Secretary of the Interior Walter Hickel to explore a "continental approach" to energy resources, an approach Greene told reporters he found "most attractive." Let's be clear: a continental approach to resources does not mean Canada and the U.S. sharing North America's bounty; it means our selling the U.S. our oil, gas, hydro and, eventually water. Greene said water had not been included in the discussion, although hydro-electric power had, but it doesn't take much imagination to see that part of any energy-resource sales packages will be our most precious resource — water.

There is nothing wrong with any of these exchanges, but before they harden into decisions, Canadians should be drawn into the debate; we must know what we are likely to be asked for and why, and what the long-term results may be.

The western and southwestern U.S. face a critical water shortage. A generally dry climate and a rate of population growth greater than the national average are pressing on inadequate reserves. Already, Arizona uses three million acre-feet of water more every year than it receives in rain, snow and river-flow (an acre-foot is the amount of water that will cover one acre to a depth of 12 inches; roughly, 326,000 gallons). The deficiency is met by "mining" underground supplies from a water table that is sinking at a rate of 20 feet per year. In Utah, according to Jay Bingham, of the Western States Water Council, "the lack of water has slowed our development to the point where we have had to resort to cannibalization. When the Geneva Steel plant went in at Provo, we got water for it by taking 1,500 acres of irrigated farmland out of production." The Colorado River, chief source of supply for the southwest, is so heavily used that virtually none of it ever reaches the Gulf of California.

If today's situation is bad, tomorrow's prospects are worse. The 17 western states, whose population now stands at 43 million, are expected to contain 108-million people by the year 2000. There will not be enough water to service them. The Western Water Development Subcommittee reported: "This water crisis is a problem of serious and far-reaching implications. It will grow steadily worse until it reaches alarming proportions in the years 1980 and 2000."

There are a number of ways in which the U.S. could meet western water problems. Current supplies could be cleaned up, redistributed and reused; these steps might not provide a permanent solution, but at least they would buy time. Desalting ocean water is another technique that might be tried; so is weather modification — seeding clouds to produce rain. But weather modification has not yet proved to be practical; desalinization is enormously expensive and has never been undertaken on anything like the scale that would be required. How much simpler, how much more natural, to look north, where water abounds, north where the stuff flows by the trillions of gallons, untasted and untouched, into the sea. North to Canada.

We have more water per capita than any nation in the world. Our freshwater supply has been estimated at anywhere from 20 to 50 percent of all the fresh water on the planet, and much of this huge volume spills unused into the oceans off our north and northwest coasts. Why not turn this northward flow back south and put it to work for the Americans, thus earning their undying gratitude, to say nothing of a fast buck?

Many schemes have been formulated to this end. The first and most famous was NAWAPA, unrolled to a deafening beat of public-relations' drums in 1964. NAWAPA is a proposal to block off parts of north-flowing Canadian and Alaskan rivers and to pump the water 1,000 feet up through huge pipelines to the Rocky Mountain trench, a 500 mile-long natural gorge containing the Columbia, Fraser and Kootenay Rivers. From here, the water would spill eastward across the Canadian prairies to the

Great Lakes, southward across the American drylands to Mexico. Hydro generated along the system would provide the push to lift the water where it was needed, and a handsome surplus to sell at a profit.

The scheme had the blessing of the U.S. Senate subcommittee, but its size, complexity and the hard sell that surrounded its launching caused Canadian politicians to shy away. Although it called for the use of less than one fifth of the north-flowing streams, the principal fact that struck Canadians about NAWAPA was that it turned our water into an American resource. Government reaction, as I have already indicated, combined public disapproval and private interest, but the plan has progressed no further than the drawing board.

Alex Davidson, Assistant Deputy Minister of the Water Branch in the Department of Energy, does not expect NAWAPA to be built, but he does expect that water export will take place, beginning with small diversions and working up to larger ones. For one of the effects of the U.S. proposal was to spawn a series of alternative plans, sons of NAWAPA. One of the least serious of these was a flat offer from Governor Ronald Reagan of California to trade us a university for some water; one of the most serious was that put forward by Lewis Smith of Denver, a water engineer with experience in the U.S., Pakistan, Ghana and Korea. Smith's plan would tap the Mackenzie River basin by turning the Liard River and sending it south; it would provide 40-million acre-feet of water, largely through existing channels.

But whether this scheme or some other is settled on, the point for Canadians is that our experts expect, one day, to see one of these plans come to life. What will happen when it does?

For one thing, Canada will make a great deal of money. No price has ever been put on water, because it has never been sold, but it is bound to be high. There will also be billions of dollars in construction costs and power sales, and whatever benefits we are able to wring out of water moving across our territory to the U.S.

A second result of any major water export will be to open areas in both Canada and the U.S. to new development. This development will be more important in the U.S. than in Canada, obviously, but the benefits to be gained from leading water across the prairies or flushing out the polluted Great Lakes should not be under-estimated.

A third result, and the one that should cause Canadians concern, will be to link our resources irrevocably to American needs. Export is a tap that, once turned on, could never be shut off again.

Without ever using the phrase "dog-in-the-manger," Senator Frank Moss of Utah hints that for Canada to hoard undeveloped supplies the U.S. needs is somehow unfair. "Frankly," he says, "there is a moral issue involved. Projecting ourselves ahead at the rate of population growth we are going to see, you would have actual privation in some areas, while in others [i.e., Canada] water is literally going to waste. And that begins to border on the moral factor."

Frankly, I can't see that morality has anything to do with it. If Americans were dying of thirst, we would have no choice; but our water will not slake American throats, it will drive American factories. What is at stake is the speed and direction of U.S. development, and it is not moral to put that development ahead of our own; it is just plain stupid. "The strongest argument opponents [of diversion] have," says Alex Davidson, "is when they ask us to prove that 200 years from now we won't need the water back. It can't be proved."

Americans already own too much of Canada. They own most of our manufacturing and nearly all of such resource-based industries as mining and petroleum. No other industrialized nation has ever been penetrated so massively by another. What is more and what is worse, the U.S. firms that dominate our economy march to drums beaten in Chicago, New York and Washington, not in Ottawa. What would happen if a difference of opinion arose over the development of a U.S.-controlled water diversion scheme? Would the Americans say, "Well, it's your water, do what you like with it"? Not bloody likely.

Another factor. If a large area of the U.S. became dependent on our water, the temptation to interfere in our domestic politics to safeguard that supply would be very great. And the U.S. track record on intervention from Santo Domingo to Saigon (and, according to former Prime Minister John Diefenbaker, even to Ottawa) has not been reassuring.

I am not suggesting here that the U.S. is engaged in an evil plot to snatch away our sovereignty. For decades, American companies have been invited, even begged, to plunder our resources. We sell, and they buy, and if our nationhood goes into the bargain that is our affair, not theirs. When we shriek that we are being savaged against our will, we are like a girl who hurls herself to the ground, hikes up her skirts and screams, "Rape!" If the process is to stop, it is we who must stop it, by ordering

our own future rather than meekly accepting theirs.

It is not enough simply to say "not now" on water export. As the need grows in the west and southwest, as economic and political pressure mounts in Washington and Ottawa, the vacuum created by our lack of policy will be filled — by the U.S. if not by us. Americans will not always be satisfied with the answer they have been getting since 1964, the answer that we are still counting our water, and will they please come back later. "I won't say you are stalling," says Utah's Senator Frank Moss, "but if it goes on much longer, some people will say that."

We're not stalling; we really don't know how much water we have or how much we may need, and we're not anxious to spend the money to find out. Energy Minister Greene explains, "With the current pressure on the Canadian tax dollar, the question of whether or not we have water to spare is not likely to receive quick attention."

That won't do. Canada must begin, now, to develop a policy on water export, a policy that acknowledges that we have a surplus but aims to make that surplus work for Canada, not the U.S. Unless we plan to develop our water resources in our own national interest, we will find, as we found with oil and nickel and iron ore, that someone else is willing to develop — and own — them for us. If capital is required from the U.S. — and it will be — it should cross the border as loans, not equity; as bonds, not stocks. If water is to be sold to the U.S. — and it will be — such sales should be made only after the last potential drop of development has been siphoned off in Canada.

It will not do to say, as our government has been saying, that we will develop a policy when the time comes. The time is now. If we wait much longer there is a good chance that our development, our prosperity, our sovereignty will disappear one dusty day down an American drain.

CANADA IS FINANCING ITS OWN SELL-OUT

Cy Gonick

Cy Gonick, an NDP member of the Manitoba legislature, is a former professor of Economics. He is editor of Canadian Dimension Magazine.

A broadly based nationalist sentiment sweeping across Canada is being met by cynicism from some and fear from others, as well as doubts, warnings (some of them legitimate) and bandwagoning among large numbers of recent converts. Out of these various reactions there have appeared many myths surrounding foreign ownership and continentalism. It is important that these myths be countered and exposed.

Myth No. 1

"Canada needs foreign capital for its economic progress"

Canada needs foreign capital. Without it we are doomed to a state of economic backwardness — a 30 per cent drop in our standard of living Prime Minister Trudeau has said. This was true for the economy of the 19th century and the early 20th century. We had a narrow economic base, and our income was too small to generate the savings needed to build the railways and the canals and all the other infrastructure that go with a newly developing economy.

Now our income is among the highest in the world — and we are one of the greatest savers in the world. We can just about finance our economic development with our own savings, and to a very large degree we already do. Despite all the talk about foreign investment, almost all investment in Canada is financed out of savings earned in Canada. But much of this money is foreign owned.

Reprinted with permission of Cy Gonick, editor of *Canadian Dimension Magazine* and NDP MLA for Crescentwood, Winnipeg, Manitoba, in *Toronto Daily Star,* November 28, 1970.

Today our problem is not a shortage of capital, but that a great deal of the money earned in Canada is foreign controlled. When it is reinvested, it allows already existing foreign companies located in Canada to expand and to buy up Canadian companies. And we call that foreign investment.

We are at a stage now where we are being bought out by our own money. The actual foreign cash makes up only a small part — in 1968, less than 15 per cent — of foreign investment in Canada. The rest of the foreign investment is done by reinvesting profits earned in Canada, deprecia-tion allowances, borrowing money from Canadian banks, and by being rewarded grants and loans from provincial and federal governments.

Conclusion: There is no economic need for more takeovers, no economic need for more foreign investment. If we can maintain a full employment level of national income, we can generate enough capital. But we have to get control over that capital. Ultimately, the only way to do that is by taking over ownership of the branch plants and foreign subsidiaries. That is the hard reality which many sentimentalists will not accept.

Myth No. 2

"The multi-national corporation is too big for Canada to fight"

We cannot resist the multi-national corporation. It's all powerful. We can't defeat it so we had better join the world of the multi-national corporations — create our own multi-national corporations and fight it out on world markets.

This sounds good. But what are the implications? The multi-national corporation is an instrument for integrating an industry on a global scale — for industry planning on a world-wide basis. What does this mean to the nation-state? The two are on a collision course. The nation-state has certain instruments to implement national policy — full employment, regional equality, price stability. The multi-national corporation can counter, neutralize and nullify these instruments.

Under the domination of the multi-national corporation the nation-state is increasingly unable to exercise real authority. For example, Ottawa has been quite unable to control inflation, largely because it is imported from the U.S.

The U.S. now owns $40 billion of assets in Canada. Where does control over these assets rest? Buying decisions, selling decisions, processing decisions, research and development decisions, investment decisions, export decisions, location decisions — they rest in the boardrooms of the parent companies. Through the multi-national corporation, foreign ownership transfers effective control from Canadian people to the executives and general managers in Detroit and New York and Philadelphia. Creating our own multi-national corporations is no solution. To do that is to run away from the problem.

The multi-national corporation is not an instrument of internationalism; it is an instrument of nationalism —

U.S. nationalism. It has a flag — the Stars and Stripes. It is used to implement American foreign policy just as the State Department is used to promote and protect the multi-national corporation. The two are inseparable.

The multi-national corporation has never helped to equalize incomes or opportunities between nations. On the contrary, it acts as a mechanism to drain the most talented and skilled and highly productive people from poor areas and to transfer them to rich areas, where the multi-national corporations are headquartered.

Ultimately, the spread of the multi-national corporation leads to the establishment of a few lead centres where the various multi-national corporations are located and where all the key economic decisions are made — and where, as a consequence, the most brilliant and innovative people are attracted.

Conclusion: To give up the struggle against the multi-national corporation is to give up the struggle for the survival of Canada as a nation-state. Moreover, there is an alternative. Instead of integrating industries on a world scale via the multi-national corporation, we could integrate industries within the nation-state via national planning. There has always been that alternative. Some people call it socialism; I think it is common sense.

Myth No. 3

"Buying back U.S.-owned firms is unrealistic and impractical"

Economic independence is fine as a principle, and certain positive steps can be taken to encourage more Canadian ownership. But "buying back" U.S.-owned companies is unrealistic, impractical and unnecessary.

I have already tried to show that future growth in Canada does not occur primarily through newly established companies or new cash flows from outside the country. It occurs largely through the reinvestment of profits earned in Canada, to a very large degree by U.S.-owned companies. Two conclusions follow from this: To allow unrestricted reinvestment of profits by U.S.-owned companies is to encourage rapid expansion of U.S. ownership in Canada regardless of what positive incentives are provided to encourage Canadian-owned industry; and to disallow or restrict reinvestment of profits earned by U.S.-owned companies would result in massive outflow of income from Canada — about $3 billion a year. This is about $1 for every $25 dollars spent by Canadians each year, and an impossible drain to contemplate on a never-ending basis.

What follows is that to avoid both continued rapid expansion of U.S. ownership and its alternative — massive and continuing outflows of money — it is absolutely necessary to begin a large-scale program of repatriation through the agency of the Crown, the only way it can be practically done.

What are the mechanics? How can we pay for it? The conventional mechanics is to replace the paper stocks which give ownership to U.S. parent companies by bonds. This transforms U.S. ownership to U.S.

loans. Ownership and control would then reside in Canada. The new owners would be newly established Crown corporations. Over a period of time they would pay off the loan with a part of the profits earned by them, profits which are flowing to the U.S. anyway and for which we now receive no equity in return. Under the new arrangement a portion of the profits would be used to pay off the loan and in the meantime Canada would exercise full sovereignty.

Conclusion: There are many problems undoubtedly overlooked by this short answer, but in general it is possible to say that repatriation of Canada's industry is possible through agencies of the Crown — i.e., public ownership — and essential as a strategy for Canadian independence.

Myth No. 4

"Foreign investment actually helps Canadian independence"

Canada is becoming more independent as it gets wealthier. Foreign investment makes us more wealthy. Therefore it contributes to our independence.

I wish it were that simple, but it is patently untrue. Foreign ownership is growing day by day. The percentage of key industries controlled from the U.S. increases at each count. Each year we lose over a billion dollars of income in order to pay for that foreign investment. And even if we stopped all foreign investment from the U.S., it would still expand and gobble up more and more of our key industries just by the existing subsidiaries reinvesting their profits. Foreign ownership automatically grows with the Canadian economy. U.S. subsidiaries are locked into Canadian economic growth. This growth provides them with the profit they need to both reward the parent company and to finance new investments in Canada.

Let's look at some of the latest figures of U.S. control (May, 1970): Iron mine industry, 85.8 per cent; oil and gas-well industry. 65 per cent; non-metal mining industry, 65 per cent; fruit and vegetable canners, 62.3 per cent; rubber products, 82.8 per cent; synthetic textiles, 7.15 per cent; publishing, 40.7 per cent; aircraft and parts industries, 48.3 per cent; motor vehicles and parts, 95.6 per cent; industrial electrical equipment, 89.6 per cent; petroleum refineries, 72 per cent: fertilizers, 49.7 per cent; pharmaceutical, 68.6 per cent; industrial chemicals, 58.9 per cent; sporting goods and toys, 51.3 per cent.

Conclusion: Foreign ownership does not lead to independence. It leads to greater and greater dependence.

Myth No. 5

**"It is in Canada's interest
to act as a resource base
for the United States"**

It is in Canada's interest to act as a resource base for the U.S. That is where we are most productive. That's where we can make the most earnings.

What is ignored by this argument is that the export of raw material is in reality the export of Canadian jobs. Resource extraction provides fewer than 100,000 jobs in Canada, but the refinery and fabrication of those resources creates millions of jobs in the U.S., Europe and Japan.

The announcement of the export of natural gas to the U.S. is only the latest example of our short-sightedness. In the short-run it creates jobs and profits; in the long-run it destroys our future. We now learn that the price of natural gas in the U.S. will almost double in the next six months. The U.S. is running out of raw materials; the costs are, therefore, rising. This puts us at a distinct advantage — perhaps for the first time.

Conclusion: If we refrain from entering into resource export deals and instead fabricated our resources here, we could be using our growing cost advantage to win a major place for ourselves among the manufacturing nations of the world — with the jobs and the incomes that go with it.

Myth No. 6

**"The answer is 51 per cent
Canadian ownership of
all firms in Canada"**

One giant obfuscation is that all would be well if only there were 51 per cent Canadian ownership of all companies doing business in Canada.

Any such mechanical formulation is superficial. Moreover, citizenship or place of residence as criteria of public policy are themselves of interest only to certain Canadian business interests who are now excluded from participating in many dynamic and profitable companies. The 51 per cent formula would force U.S. companies to make greater room for Canadian capitalists.

But the citizenship or place of residence of the owners of Canadian industry has only a minor bearing on the well-being of ordinary Canadians. What *is* of vital importance to the well-being of ordinary Canadians is the economic subordination of Canada to the U.S. via U.S. corporate ownership of Canadian industry. That Canada has become a resource base for U.S. industry is important; that Canada has become a sub-region of the U.S. consumer market fashioned by Madison Ave. is important; that our lives are now glutted with U.S. housing styles, textbooks, television, entertainment patterns, thoughts — all of this is vitally important.

U.S. values of possessive individualism are transferred to Canada through

the media, the goods we make, the goods we consume, and seep inside our lives until we become miniature replicas of the Americans. Because we have become attached to the U.S. as an economic and cultural colony, our standard of comparison is naturally the U.S. We come to judge ourselves in terms of our success in catching up to and living like and being like the Americans. We come to be a totally derivative society — imitators not innovators. And then we worry and fret that the Canadian identity is being lost.

What is important is not the citizenship and place of residence, it is the fact that with the economic subordination to the U.S. that stems from American ownership, we become attached to America, an economic satellite of and a cultural colony to the U.S. We become like Americans. We lose the potential of becoming something different. What is also important is that U.S. ownership transfers effective control away from the Canadian people.

The access to U.S. corporate directorships by Canadian capitalists to the extent of 51 per cent is most unlikely to change any of this. The continental economic structure would probably be unaffected; the north-south trade flows would not decrease; the technological dependence would continue; the emphasis on raw material export would not alter. Real decisons would still emanate from the U.S. The overwhelming importance of the multi-national corporation would be untouched.

The only effect of the 51 per cent Canadian ownership condition would be that some profits would be transferred from U.S. capitalists to Canadian capitalists, and that the terms of trade may be more favorable to Canada.

In any event, it is most unlikely that the 51 per cent formula is even workable. First, there probably isn't sufficient willing private Canadian capital to buy 51 per cent equity. Second, the subsidiaries would retain control by dividing the 51 per cent shares into many, many small holdings and keeping the biggest holdings (49 per cent). Third, although this formula is of interest to some Canadian businessmen, it scares most of them who are unwilling to stir up the U.S. giant over this issue. The majority of Canada's economic elite is satisfied with what they are getting out of the U.S. relationship.

Conclusion: The 51 per cent ownership condition sounds radical at first hearing, but it turns out to be largely irrelevant to Canadian independence and of primary benefit only to that section of Canadian business which feels excluded from lucrative positions in U.S.-owned corporations. Moreover, it is doubtful whether the majority of Canada's economic elite would support this demand. They are worried that it will anger the Americans, cause them to withdraw their concessions — all of which would jeopardize their own profits and prestige which depend, to an increasing degree, on the presence of U.S. branch plantism and continentalist structures. It is utter folly to suggest that development policy would be more in the public interest with Canadian corporate men at the helm. But capitalism in Canada is now predominantly American, and that is why foreign ownership and not just the corporate system is relevant. The corporate system in Canada is Americanized. The two cannot be separated.

Myth No. 7

"The answer is that foreign firms be good corporate citizens of Canada"

It is argued that there is nothing wrong with foreign ownership per se, providing foreign companies operate as "good corporate citizens" of Canada.

This argument confuses performance with structure. The performance of branch plants may or may not be as satisfactory as the performance of Canadian-owned companies. There is some evidence that they consistently under-price their exports to parent companies and that they over-import from their parent companies.

But the real issue is not their comparative performance. It is the kind of economic structure that their presence assures, a structure in which both Canadian-owned and U.S.-owned companies must operate. It is this structure that is inefficient. It reduces Canada to a resource base of the U.S., and makes Canada totally dependent on decisions made in the U.S.

Foreign ownership is undesirable not only because it transfers decisions out of Canada, but because it is the primary instrument which binds Canada to the U.S. — economically and culturally. It makes us a satellite of the U.S., dependent upon the U.S. regardless of which citizens make the decisions. Given the present economic structure of continentalism, it is in the interest of Canadian industrialists to perpetuate the north-south trade and to do nothing to stop the erosion of Canadian sovereignty. For any such measures would disrupt their own profitable relationship with the U.S.

But this argument is fallacious in another sense. "Bad corporate citizenship" may be somewhat of a problem — loss of markets in Cuba, China, etc., and other behavior collectively known as "extraterritoriality." But the real problem lies with good corporate citizenship.

Car manufacturers, for example, through sales promotion, fill our minds with envy, greed and want. They appeal to every dimension of our psyche — our sexual needs, our sense of inferiority, our sense of superiority, our need to be accepted, our lust for status.

And the result of their success? Cities that are deformed, noisy, crowded, filthy, ugly; streets that are unwalkable; and billions and billions of dollars a year spent on parking, highways, expressways, repair, to say nothing of the cars themselves—while real needs of people still go unmet. This is good corporate citizenship.

The normal behavior of any business is to use whatever techniques are available to sell and to win as big a portion of the total market and the total resources of an economy as possible. It is, in short, the profit system. What is also normal corporate citizenship is the laying off of workers as markets weaken; the abandoning of plants as profits sag; the introduction of new technology regardless of its consequences on jobs. Even if it were possible to achieve an independent Canada without altering the profit system, a proposition that I would completely reject, being good corporate citizens of Canada is barely better than being good corporate citizens of the U.S.

Conclusion: Insisting on good corporate citizenship is irrelevant as far as Canadian independence is concerned. It will not make Canada more independent. It will not change Canada from a resource colony of the U.S. However, good corporate citizenship is also irrelevant as a standard of measuring the wellbeing of the Canadian people. The problem is not bad corporate citizenship, but corporate citizenship itself—which happens to be centered in the U.S. as the leader of the capitalist world. There is no meaningful choice between bad corporate citizenship and good corporate citizenship. The difference between them is trivial. The meaningful choice is corporate capitalism or democratic socialism.

Myth No. 8

"Canada needs U.S. investment to offset its trade imbalance"

U.S. investment is needed to offset Canada's trade deficit on current account of our balance of payment. We import more from the United States than we export to it. We have to find U.S. dollars to make up the difference. That is why we must have U.S. investment.

We do have a large deficit on current account. But the biggest reason for the deficit is the huge dividends and interest we have to pay each year for past foreign investments — to the tune of over a billion dollars a year plus royalties, management fees and the like.

Connected with the establishment of branch plants is the large-scale importation of materials and parts from parent companies. Foreign ownership automatically leads to closer trade ties between the two countries. And that explains to a very large degree why 75 per cent of our imports come from the U.S., and why we do have a large trade deficit with the U.S. We have a surplus on capital account caused by the expansion of foreign investment. Naturally this has to be offset by a deficit on current accounts and it takes the form of an outflow of dollars — dividends and interest, royalties, etc., and a trade deficit.

Conclusion: Foreign investment is not required to close a trade deficit. The trade deficit and the net outflow of dollars to the U.S. is largely abused by foreign investment and the establishment of branch plants.

Myth No. 9

"Foreign investment helps Canada obtain foreign technology"

We need foreign capital because with it we get the foreign technology we would otherwise have to pay for.

Let's look at the facts. Industrial technology is generated in industrial laboratories, especially in the labs of the most highly dynamic and technically complex industries. All of these industries in Canada are dominated by U.S. companies. They do virtually all their basic research in the labs of the parent companies in the U.S. If Canadian scientists want work in in-dustrial research, they often have to go to the U.S. Foreign ownership causes us to export our potential technicians after paying for their training. We lose the very people who would be able to develop our technology.

Conclusion: Foreign capital brings with it foreign technology, yes, but it also causes the loss of potential Canadian technology. We get the technology made to measure for Chicago and Detroit, New York and Philadelphia, which is then imposed on our cities and by necessity transforms our cities. At the same time we lose the capacity to create technology relevant to our specific needs.

Myth No. 10

"Economic nationalism is futile, dangerous and anti-American"

Economic nationalism is isolationist, parochial, dangerous, futile and anti-American.

What I have tried to show up to now is that economic domination of Canada by the U.S. is unnecessary. I have agreed that if we had the will, the courage, the guts, we could be far more self-determining. That should be our goal if we are democrats. We should be interested in being free to shape our own lives. To be less than fanatical about controlling our own future, our own destiny, is to be less than human.

We have to define ourselves in terms of the U.S. But not just us — every nation in the Western world. Because the U.S. is swallowing all of us up. She is like all other empires that have depleted their own resources and glutted their own markets. She must expand and expand and expand until entire continents become her resource base and her consumer markets. And as she expands and absorbs, she spreads not only her technology, her goods and her armies, but also her culture, her ideas, her way of life. It is the way of all empires.

To resist Americanization is not futile. Nor does it lead to Auschwitz, which is what so many liberal intellectuals think of when they think of nationalism. Nationalism in Canada means resistance to U.S. imperialism. It is the greatest of ironies that these cosmopolitans — these internationalists who quake at the thought of Canadian nationalism — are quite willing to see Canada joining with the most dangerous nationalism that exists today, the nationalism of the U.S. That's what internationalism for Canada means today.

It is too easy for us who are critical of this drift, who say we will not tolerate it, to pound away at the Americans. We have to accept America for what she has become; the greatest imperial giant of the 20th century. What we need not accept — what we must not accept — are the men who lead this country of ours into this unnecessary alliance. The Americans move into Canada and take our resources because we do not know what we want to do with them. And she gluts our markets and our media with Americana because we cannot decide what we want to be. We have no plans; we have no designs. The Americans do. They ran out of resources. They needed our markets.

They used us — our resources, our manpower, our brains — to help them achieve their goal. And we didn't resist, because we had no goal of our own. It wasn't rape; we volunteered enthusiastically.

Why didn't we resist? Why don't we resist? Because, in my view, we are led by a class in Canada that profits from continentalism, that profits from takeovers, that profits from resource removal. This class, this economic elite, has decided that it is in its interest to see Canada remain a satellite of the U.S. It is this class, and its allies in the press, in politics, in the academies of learning, that have decided that continentalism is necessary and that independence is impossible.

George Grant has written that "the economic self-seekers have never been the ones to care about Canada as a nation." It is evident to me that they will never assert that Canada is not for sale. It is evident to me that they will only ask, "What price is being offered?"

THE STRUCTURE
OF CANADIAN INDUSTRY—

Report of the Task Force on the Structure of Canadian Industry

Percentage of total owned or controlled by all non-residents	Non-resident ownership			Non-resident control		
	1926	1948	1963	1926	1948	1963
Manufacturing	38	42	54	35	43	60
Petroleum and natural gas	—	—	64	—	—	74
Mining and smelting	37	39	62	38	40	59
Railways	55	45	23	3	3	2
Other utilities	32	20	13	20	24	4
Total of above industries and merchandising	37	32	35	17	25	34

Percentage of total owned or controlled by U.S. residents	Non-resident ownership			Non-resident control		
	1926	1948	1963	1926	1948	1963
Manufacturing	30	35	44	30	39	46
Petroleum and natural gas	—	—	54	—	—	62
Mining and smelting	28	32	54	32	37	52
Railways	15	21	9	3	3	2
Other utilities	23	16	23	20	24	4
Total of above industries and merchandising	19	23	28	15	22	27

Reprinted from Foreign Ownership and the Structure of Canadian Industry: Report of the Task Force on the Structure of Canadian Industry, prepared for the Privy Council Office. Reproduced with the permission of Information Canada.

AN ACT OF LUNACY:

Book Publishing in Canada

Peter Martin

Peter Martin is the founder of Peter Martin Associates Ltd., book publishers.

If the Americans dealt in rasbukniks and spoke Urdu, I'd be all right — maybe. But since they deal in dollars and speak English, I've got troubles.

I'm a Canadian book publisher. Founder (with my wife, who is really the brains of the outfit) and president of a middle-sized, middle-aged Canadian-owned book publishing house.

We've been in business for seven years now, which makes us a senior citizen among the dozen or so new publishing houses which have sprung up in Canada in the last decade. During those years, we've published pretty close to forty original Canadian books and we're now producing between ten and fifteen new titles a year.

None of our books has been a really big bestseller of the Arthur Hailey or Pierre Berton variety, but some have done pretty well. Perhaps you've heard of a few of them? *Canadian Real Estate: How to Make it Pay* by Richard Steacy. *Killing Ground,* a novel about a war between Quebec and Canada, by Ellis Portal. Or perhaps *Yellowknife* or *The Howling Arctic* by Ray Price. All good books, well written, and designed to entertain and inform Canadian readers.

Some of our other successful titles I'm almost certain you haven't heard about. *Lucile Panabaker's Song Book* is a text that's admired, respected and used across both Canada and the United States; Miss Panabaker, from Kitchener, Ontario, is one of the continent's leading experts on musical education for pre-school children. Or John Kolasky's *Two Years in Soviet Ukraine;* we've sold pretty close to 10,000 copies (technically, bestseller status) of this remarkable inside account of Russian carpetbagger imperialism in the Ukraine. Both these books enhanced our reputation and turned a neat profit, but you're not likely to see either of them featured in your neighbourhood bookshop.

Of course, we've had our failures too. Books launched with great expectations, only to die, unwanted and unmourned (except by their authors — and us!).

But on balance, we've been doing pretty well. Finding or commissioning good manuscripts, editing them effectively, having them manufactured efficiently and attractively, and then

Reprinted with permission of Peter Martin and The Canadian Banker, March/April 1971.

marketing them with the necessary mix of aggressive tub-thumping and cool concern for a return on the dollar.

So there we are. Peter Martin Associates Limited. A good, solid little Canadian book publishing house with a growing backlist of successful books and great prospects for the future. Firms like ours don't produce any fortunes overnight; in book publishing you have to be there for the long haul — the Macmillan Company was in business for a century or so, after all, before they contributed their first prime minister to Great Britain. But fortunes aside, a firm like ours is a nice, solid citizen with, other things being equal, a good long-term future.

Why then, you might very well ask, did Peter Martin Associates almost go into receivership at the end of last year? And, for that matter, why did the W. J. Gage Company sell its textbook division to an American firm in September and the United Church turn over the Ryerson Press to Mc-Graw-Hill in November? Why did Jack McClelland, the flamboyant owner of McClelland and Stewart, the largest of the remaining Canadian publishing houses, announce at a press conference in February that his company was for sale? Why has House of Anansi, one of my more exciting competitors and a firm responsible for about 50 per cent of the new fiction published in Canada in the past few years, cut its publishing program back to about a quarter of its 1969 and 1970 level?

The simple answer, of course, is that attempting to publish books in Canada is, *prima facie*, an act of absolute lunacy.

But, as always, the simple answer is worse than no answer at all. The Canadian book publishing industry is in trouble — but not, by and large, because its practitioners are either incompetent or insane.

We're in trouble because the Americans speak English and price their products in dollars.

Because Canada is completely open to the importation and sale of American and, to a lesser extent, British books (and I don't know a book publisher who wants a tough tariff; we all, to a man, believe that the flow of thought and ideas should not be impeded by national boundaries), Canadian book publishers are in direct competition in the Canadian market with their counterparts in the other two major English-speaking countries.

A chronic hunger for working capital is not, of course, a uniquely Canadian phenomenon among book publishers. Publishers everywhere face the same problems; they have to manufacture their products in "batches" instead of "on stream" and they have to carry heavy inventories of expensive, unsold product. Books in inventory appear on the balance sheet as an asset — they can, after all, be counted, kicked, squeezed and otherwise assessed by the auditors and the moneylenders. But inventory often *feels* like a liability to the publisher. That's slow-moving (or maybe dead!) money back there in the warehouse. What is particularly frustrating for the publisher is that his *real* assets never appear on the balance sheet. Oh, perhaps there's a provision for "goodwill", but everyone knows you ignore that item when you're assessing a company's strength. But, for a book publisher, something like "goodwill" represents his only really important assets. These intangible assets are a complex and shifting mixture of contracts, options, licences, friendships, ideas, possibilities. They are, from one viewpoint, summed up in his personal relationships with his "stable" of writers. The publisher's most important work is not done when he attempts to explain to his banker why his accounts receivable are coming in so slowly; it's done when he buys a beer for a young writer he believes in and encourages the writer to get on with his new book, or when he gets an idea himself for a book and goes out and finds somebody to write it, or when he accepts a manuscript from a writer with no track record at all just because he *knows* it's good, or important — or salable!

In the United States there has been a remarkable recognition of the real role of the publisher. Book publishers are not primarily merchants of "hardware" — sellers of manufactured products called books — but are instead creators of "software"—assiduous tillers of the soil in which new ideas can grow and flourish. When this fact was recognized on Wall Street, the giants of the communications world moved in on the book publishers. Time-Life acquired Little, Brown. IBM picked up Science Research Associates. RCA bought Bennett Cerf's Random House. Litton Industries moved in on Van Nostrand Reinhold. All the large corporate buyers — who paid very high earning multiples for their acquisitions — knew they were buying something with values that didn't show up on the balance sheets; they were picking up the publishers' competence as software generators. McLuhan notwithstanding, communications enterprises have to find some message to fill the pipeline of the medium. And the book publishers, who had been at it for centuries, were recognized as experts at finding, developing and packaging messages.

That's what happened in New York. In Canada, all that happened was that the American book publishing subsidiaries found themselves sud-denly the beneficiaries of management expertise and essentially unlimited working capital and credit flowing through from the new rich owners of their American parents.

As for the Canadian owned publishing houses . . . their difficulties multiplied and their position deteriorated; they weren't getting new money from the multicorp giants, but they were competing with foreign-based houses which were.

The Americans, ironically, have carefully protected their own domestic book market from foreign competition for the last hundred years or so. Congress wrote into American copyright law an iniquitous provision which came to be known as the "manufacturing clause". It said that any book in the English language imported into the United States in quantities of more than 1,500 copies lost all American copyright protection. The purpose of the "manufacturing clause" was simply to protect American printers from cheap foreign competition. But its effect was to close the American market to books edited and produced in Canada.

In 1962, the Americans modified the "manufacturing clause". Now Canadian and other non-American publishers only stand to lose copyright protection if the author is an American citizen.

But the damage had been done. Canadian publishers and printers had learned that they simply had no access to the vast American market. The Americans, of course, had learned exactly the opposite truth about the Canadian market. For Canadian publishers, the barrier against export to the United States is now largely psychological; but often psychological barriers are the hardest ones to break through.

Since British books have managed

to hold onto only about 12 per cent of the Canadian market, the Americans are the dominant influence. In effect, they set the prices.

And that's why I wish they'd stop using dollars and speaking English.

Consider a hypothetical case. A New York publisher (Great American Books, a wholly-owned subsidiary of Giant Universal Conglomerated Everything, Inc., a Delaware corporation, which can flow unlimited capital through to its book publishing subsidiary because of its depletion allowances on its off-shore oil operations in the Gulf of Mexico) announces a new book of wide, general interest. The book is, let's say, "Better Bank Loans at Half the Cost". The price of the book is set at $6.95. The first printing is 30,000 copies. And $50,000 is allocated for promotion (Great American, remember, has lots of capital).

The book is reviewed in *Time, Fortune* and *Newsweek*. It's condensed in the *Reader's Digest*. The author appears on all those late-night talk shows that Canadians watch if they're close to the border or on cable.

In the States, "Better Bank Loans" goes onto the bestseller list. Great American goes back to press with another 50,000 copies. Great American of Canada Limited imports 5,000 copies from New York and the book does pretty well in Canada, too (astonishing as it might seem, our banks being so different from their American counterparts, but Canadians are very agile at translating the American experience into our own).

Meanwhile, what are we up to at Peter Martin Associates?

Well, as it happens, we're bringing out a book called "Better Canadian Bank Loans . . . " We're pricing it at $7.50. We don't have the capital to promote it heavily. And we're selling it to a market with 21 million people in it, instead of the 230 million market our rich New York competitor has to work with. Our price is a little higher than his, but we can't go too much higher because Canadians *know* what books should cost them; they read the American reviews and that's how they know.

Our first printing is 3,000 copies. At a unit manufacturing cost of $2.00 a book, that means we have put $6,000 into our book.

If it performed like a typical Peter Martin Associates nonfiction title, we'd sell 2,500 copies in the first twelve months after publication and we'd gross $4.50 a copy (the publisher sells to the bookstores at a discount that averages out at around 40 per cent of list price).

Now, here's what happens to our sales dollar. Forty cents goes to the typesetters, printers and binders for manufacturing. Seventeen cents goes to the author as royalties. Fifteen cents is spent on promotion, catalogues and advertising. And about twenty-five cents is a contribution to general overhead to pay our editorial, design and production people, and to take care of general housekeeping — warehousing, shipping, billings, collections, that sort of thing.

That leaves us with a profit of 3 cents on the sales dollar.

Not too bad. The supermarkets, after all, work on lower net margins than that and they do all right (until, that is, they play the price war game).

But wait. Remember, we printed 3,000 copies and sold 2,500. That means we're carrying 500 copies in inventory. At $2.00 each, that's a thousand dollars worth of inventory we'll carry forward into next year.

On paper we've netted 3 per cent of $4.50 on 2,500 copies sold. That works out to $337.50. We're able to finance only about a third of that inventory out of retained earnings; the rest has to come from somewhere. The shareholders' invested capital? For a while. Bank loans? No. In my experience, bankers look at publishers' inventories with the kind of active distaste they'd show if I tried to borrow money on fish that had been sitting in the sun for a couple of weeks. Supplier credit? Well, yes, up to a point, but only to a point (we reached that point late last year; remember that brush with receivership I mentioned above?).

There is, in short, no ready source of capital for a Canadian book publisher. Oh sure, there's money around, but when you go looking for the funny money you find yourself paying interest rates that a 3 per cent net margin on sales can't support — and besides you're likely to have your kneecaps broken with a baseball bat when you miss a payment.

So what can we do? Raise prices? No, because the pricing environment we operate in is set in New York where they speak English, trade in dollars and produce at lower unit-cost (because their production runs are longer). Reduce the printing quantity so that there's no inventory to carry forward? No, because unit costs go up as you cut the production run and that little profit margin vanishes. Increase printing quantities to force down unit costs and increase the net profit on sales? No, obviously, because then we end with a heavier inventory carry-forward.

Maybe we should print all our books as "cheap" paperbacks? That's a suggestion that is made with discouraging frequency by people outside the industry. The truth is that wrapping a book in paper covers instead of hard covers and a jacket produces only a cost saving of about 15 per cent — but you are expected (again because of the psychology of book pricing) to reduce the retail price as much as 75 per cent. The unit cost of books goes down not by reducing the physical quality of the product, but by undertaking longer production runs. The paperbacks you look at in the local cigar store cost as little as 75 cents *not* because they're in paper covers but because they're "mass market" books, produced in quantities of 50,000 and more. And the mass market distribution system in Canada, incidentally, is almost totally dominated by American production; Canadian publishers who have tried to break into it have always been badly burned.

Since the sale of Ryerson Press, the publishers have sought another solution. We've been talking to both the federal and provincial governments in an effort to put together a program of low cost-loans or loan guarantees which would enable publishers, who meet other reasonable criteria of efficiency and good management, to borrow the money they need to supplement their working capital.

Curiously, everybody in the Canadian publishing industry is confident of the long-term prospects we face. We've got everything going for us over the long haul. Canadians are becoming increasingly interested in their own nation, its problems and its opportunities, so our product is increasingly in demand. And population, disposable incomes and average educational attainment levels are all rising in Canada and should continue to do so for the rest of this century, all indices which lead to greater demand for and consumption of books.

In the short term, however, we're in the most appalling kind of trouble, the kind of trouble that finds you staring at the ceiling at four in the morning and saying "good luck!" when you hand your employees their pay cheques. The kind of trouble that would lead a normal businessman in a normal business to close his doors and look for something else to do.

But book publishers don't behave like normal businessmen. Partly because we are all patriots and we believe that, although the book industry's share of the GNP is vanishingly small, nevertheless it's *important* that the Canadian story be told, the Canadian issues be debated, between the covers of books.

And partly, too, because we're inveterate optimists. One really big bestseller can knock all that dismal arithmetic I laid out earlier into a cocked hat, and it's hard for a publisher not to think that the next book he brings out is going to be that big bestseller.

It isn't, you see, that every book that should be written and published in Canada has already appeared. There are thousands of books still to be published in Canada and there always will be as long as Canada remains a vital, growing society.

WHERE HAS ALL OUR BEST LAND GONE? GUESS

Douglas Marshall

Douglas Marshall is a frequent contributor to Maclean's.

William J. Wineberg is an American mini-tycoon who controls a multimillion-dollar web of family corporations from a push-button grange near Portland, Oregon. The world of commerce is very much with him despite the bucolic setting. Getting and spending in a series of curt telephone calls — "Tell him he can have one minute" — he seems to recharge his powers. As the decisions snap and crackle into the receiver, he gazes contentedly out across coddled lawns undulating down past lilacs and fine old pines to the

waters of, appropriately, the Columbia River.

The Columbia has played a significant role in Wineberg's life. He was born 69 years ago in a log cabin built a few miles upstream by his parents, pioneers from Scandinavia. His fortune was founded during the Depression when, starting with $150, he began buying up properties along the lower reaches of the Columbia that were being sold for taxes. One such property, purchased for $30,000 in 1942, is now wanted by the State of Washington for parkland. The state is prepared to pay Wineberg $881,000 for its own lack of foresight.

Reprinted by permission of *Maclean's* and Douglas Marshall, from the issue of October, 1970.

That deal should be of more than passing interest to prudent Canadians because Wineberg also has a considerable stake in the water-rich wilderness where the Columbia rises. Since 1938 he has been collecting bits and pieces of the British Columbia heartland. Most of these properties were picked up for $10 an acre or less at tax sales. "We have bought islands for $400 or $500 and sold them for $40,000 or more," says Wineberg. "Nearly all the buyers are Americans. They know the value of this land. We do about $70,000 worth of real-estate business up there each year. We could sell five times that much but we don't advertise. This thing is more of a hobby for us."

At the moment Wineberg holds clear and perfect title to more than 600 parcels of undeveloped land, most of them in the Prince George area. This represents a fragmented colonial empire of some 60,000 acres. He is almost certainly the biggest individual owner of private vacation property in BC. And he's still buying. The chances are the Province of British Columbia, like the State of Washington before it, will some day soon be forced to do business with Wineberg.

Wineberg is undoubtedly a smooth operator, fast-thinking and beneath his surface amiability about as friendly as a fox. "He's a dynamic cuss," says an admiring business assistant. "He moves so quickly it's hard to keep up with him." To the Maple dewy eyes of some nationalists, he seems to be the perfect prototype of the greedy Yankee villains who have been grabbing all our precious recreational land. But there's another side to that picture. "Canadians are jealous of me and Americans like me," says Bill Wineberg, "because they've been too dumb to invest in their own country." The truth is the Americans have *not*

been stealing our priceless heritage. For years now, ever since the motorcar opened up Canada's blue lakes and rocky shores to the continental masses, we've virtually been giving it away. Until recently we've been too lazy and unimaginative, too willing to believe the myth about "unlimited resources," too ready to make a fast buck — the greediness works both ways — to care much. Now a combination of what should have been predictable circumstances are converting Canadian apathy into less-than-righteous indignation.

Before 1960 American ownership of our cottage land was mainly concentrated in a few border beachheads — the Magog area of Quebec's Eastern Townships, the Thousand Islands, the northeast shore of Lake Erie. Then in the mid-1960s, the United States suddenly ran out of reasonably priced vacation space. "Sportsmen in the U.S. are reduced to fishing carp out of cess pools," says CBC outdoors broadcaster Larry Johnston. "In terms of recreational facilities, we're holding all the aces."

Meanwhile the urban revolution, with its allied congestion problems, is creating an unprecedented demand for breathing space among Canadians themselves. Newly affluent city dwellers, cooped up in highrise cubicles for much of the year, seek properties where they can escape for the summer. The less affluent merely want an unpolluted public beach where they can enjoy a day's swim. Often they find the Stars and Stripes flying above the choice spots — with No Trespass signs and barbed wire sometimes reinforcing the territorial imperative. The bitterness this can generate is symbolized by the annual battle of the beaches at the eastern end of Lake Erie. Only 8.1 miles of the 46-mile waterfront between Port Colborne and

Fort Erie are open to the public. Americans own — and barricade themselves inside — an estimated 85% of the private property in the area. Canadians have taken to staging increasingly hostile demonstrations aimed at opening all Lake Erie beaches to the public.

Similar conflicts are shaping up elsewhere as U.S. property buyers thrust deeper into Canada on three main fronts — through the Maritimes, Ontario and BC. (There is little evidence of American interest in vacation land on the Prairies, although farmers complain that huge tracts of agricultural land near the border are falling into U.S. hands, and Newfoundland is more worried about Americans *leaving* as they close up their military bases. A special problem exists in Quebec. Few Americans purchase property in the province but many of Quebec's 1,600 private hunting and fishing clubs are operated by U.S. residents. These clubs control some 23,500 square miles of crown land under a leasing arrangement that closes off nearly 80% of the best recreational areas to the public.)

One striking factor about this three-pronged American advance on the Canadian backwoods is that nobody, including the various provincial government departments responsible for recreational land, knows precisely how far it has penetrated. Accurate figures on foreign ownership would require tedious title searches through countless thousands of local registry offices. But at least three provinces, Nova Scotia, New Brunswick and Prince Edward Island, are sufficiently alarmed to have commissioned surveys that will give them a better idea of how much of Canada is still Canadian. And the Ontario government has promised it will prepare a similar study.

Preliminary results of the Nova Scotia survey indicate that at least 10,000 landowners reside outside the province. The government won't know until the end of the year how many of these outsiders are American. But aroused natives, particularly in Cape Breton where a growing American presence and local pride mix about as naturally as bourbon and rum, are betting that at least 50% of the deeds to nonresident properties will turn out to have U.S. addresses.

Throughout the Maritime provinces there's a sense of urgency about the invasion. "American ownership of island land is a very serious concern here," says PEI's Andrew Wells, executive assistant to Premier Alex Campbell. "Our committee inquiring into the problem is also charged with making suitable recommendations to deal with it." Nova Scotia's Robert Burgess, deputy minister of lands and forests, says his province will certainly take action "if it appears that foreigners own thousands of acres in prime recreational areas and our own residents are being deprived of the use of those areas and shorelines."

The Ontario government's response to the American threat has been much more lackadaisical. For one thing, Ontario still sells crown land to non-Canadians. Last May the provincial cabinet approved the sale of 60 acres in Nipissing (at $15 an acre) to an American from Michigan who already owned 300 acres in the province. Earlier in May Premier John Robarts had promised "a very broad survey" of recreational lands to determine the extent of U.S. ownership. Yet the survey had not been started by mid-July. Meanwhile Rene Brunelle, provincial minister of lands and forests, estimates that some 40,000 of the present 315,000 cottage properties in Ontario are owned by Americans.

Brunelle's estimate hardly tells the full story, as Liberal and NDP critics in the legislature have been quick to point out. It doesn't reveal, for instance, that the rate of American purchases has increased by 15% in recent years. Nearly one fifth of the 1,065 waterfront lots sold by the province in 1969 went to U.S. residents. Moreover, the government isn't discouraging this trend. American cottage owners in Ontario (George Romney, millionaire cabinet minister in the Nixon administration, has a place near Sarnia) are said to have fallen off their private docks with laughter on learning they qualify for the province's basic $30-plus rebate on property taxes. "This is impossible to justify," thundered the Toronto *Daily Star*, noting that the original purpose of the rebate was to provide relief for hard-pressed homeowners and tenants.

Critics of Ontario's indiscriminate land policy are more disturbed by the fact that the race already seems half lost for the new generation of Canadian property hunters. Heavily populated southern Ontario, with a hinterland matched only by the Isles of Greece for terraqueous beauty, is now 90% privately owned. Liberal MPP Richard Smith estimates that Americans control as much as 50% of the cottage properties along the Ontario shorelines of the lower Great Lakes. Inland lake frontage is either all gone or going fast at $40 a foot as far north as Haliburton.

Canadians who venture into more remote parts of Ontario often discover the trails to the best properties have already been blazed by Americans. They find themselves playing the role of camp followers to an army of occupation. Opposition MPPs say that in the far west of the province, around Fort Frances and Kenora, 80% of the public land is going to U.S. residents. Americans are also buying up large sections of marginal land in this rugged Shield country — either at tax sales or by offering prices farmers can't resist. Lloyd Johnson, a Duluth lawyer, has managed to assemble 12,300 acres in the Pigeon River district near Thunder Bay during the last 35 years. The province expropriated 2,300 acres for a park seven years ago, but negotiations over payment are still dragging on. Says Johnson, "There have been suggestions that I jumped in there as a speculator, but the fact is I saw the value of the land before anyone else."

Americans, recognizing that the enticing Ontario north is only a short planetrip away from such stifling centres as Chicago and Detroit, are also investing heavily in the resort and outfitting industry. Along Ontario's Highway 71, between Fort Frances and Kenora, eight out of 10 tourist camps are U.S. owned and a Canadian license plate is a rarity. Manitoulin Island, lying off the north shore of Lake Huron, is turning into an extension of Michigan. This makes Malcolm Kirk, resources manager of the conservation authority in Owen Sound, fume: "The government did a study of the recreational potential of the Manitoulin area a year ago and published it, along with maps showing the choice spots. Now the speculators don't even have to do their own research. Americans are very eager to buy in Manitoulin. They pay as much as $500 an acre in northern Michigan and $200 an acre here looks like a great bargain. Manitoulin, unhappily, could become a rich American playground."

In British Columbia, would-be American purchasers are beginning to find the atmosphere much chillier than in central Canada. Residents in the Kootenay district last year mounted a campaign to give Canadians first chance to buy 50,000 acres of attractive waterfront property created by the Columbia River project. U.S. visitors had shown a hungry interest in the area, offering as much as $5,000 for a single acre. As a result of the campaign, the BC government recently introduced legislation that restricts the sale of crown land to Canadians only, although foreigners may still lease it. But Ran Harding, NDP MP for Kootenay West, says it is too easy for Americans to get around the new regulations. "Nothing prevents Americans from buying private property. So when they see some crown land they want, all they do is get a friend or an agent to buy it, hold it a while and then transfer it."

Harding wants the government to put a freeze on leasing, as well as purchase, of crown lands until the regional areas have enough space for parks. He would also like to see restrictions on the sale of private property. "Across the border in Washington," he says, "Canadians can't own state *or* private land. Doggone it, it seems to me there's nothing wrong with getting the same legislation up here."

Down at the other end of the Columbia, Bill Wineberg is feeling a little hurt by all this new hostility. As he flicks fondly through the 16 fat record books describing his BC holdings — "Here's a little piece we picked up for $1,500; I see it's now assessed at $30,-000"—he wonders whether Canadians aren't getting "just a bit too chintzy." He particularly resents the fact that custom officials and the RCMP have been making him pay duty on the camping equipment and cottage furniture he brings into the country. Last winter, he claims, the RCMP even went so far as to search one of his cottages while he wasn't

there. Worse, he says, customs officers confiscated the brochures advertising Wineberg's $750,000 lodge on Stuart Lake near Fort St. James, because the brochures had been printed in the U.S.

"Now that's harassment plain and simple," says Wineberg. "They don't seem to realize the lodge brings in $1,000,000 worth of business a year. Half the people up there are mad at us and condemn the locals who work for us. They treat us kindly to our face but knock us behind our backs. I can't understand why Canadians welcome hippies and deserters, the rats leaving the sinking ship, yet are jealous of solid citizens who want to invest.

"Don't get me wrong. I think of Canada as a coming country. I've encouraged dozens of Americans to buy up there. They buy because they keep seeing fertile land that looks like a steal. The air is clean, the waters are unpolluted and they can live without interference. They also see a rare opportunity for making money."

Wineberg's methods of making money out of BC are absurdly simple. He maintains a small office in Victoria staffed by one woman. Her duty is to prepare reports on the best properties going for taxes. Then Wineberg or a member of his family makes a trip to Canada to bid at the auctions personally. "We always go into a sale with first-class information — maps, aerial photos, everything. Until recently we employed a man in the provincial land office to supply further details. The reason I like to go to tax sales myself is because I've got a lot of them bluffed out up there."

Wineberg's major rival in the tax-sale field is Canada's H. M. Dignam Corporation Ltd., one of several Toronto-based firms busily engaged in selling Canada to Americans. Some firms, such as the Dignam company, buy up land auctioned for taxes and then resell it. Others simply sell information about impending sales. All advertise extensively in U.S. publications. "Buy Canada!" says a pamphlet distributed in the U.S. by one firm. "Claim your bonanza right away! Speculators, guarantee profit or money refunded."

The Dignam corporation mails out about 40,000 free booklets a year describing the properties it has acquired. Subscribers order their lots by mail. For instance, earlier this year $65 down and 20 monthly payments of $40 would have secured title to 80 acres of "picturesque and rugged land, not really suitable for modern farming" near Thunder Bay. The booklet is clearly aimed at Americans. Dignam manager David Mullin defends his operation stoutly: "I can't see any reason for prohibiting the sale of land to Americans. They pay taxes, employ local labor and buy local material. Some townships would be in a very sorry state if it weren't for the Americans."

The question remains, why aren't more Canadians cashing in on these bargains? The answer many Canadians give is that they can't afford them. Columnist Alan Dawson, writing in the Toronto *Globe and Mail,* scoffs at this argument. "Don't give me that stuff about the rich Americans and the poor Canadians. Look at the homes, the jumping night spots, the cottages, the $5,000 boats or two snowmobiles rolling along behind the big cars in Canada. There are thousands and thousands of Canadians who can easily afford the best hunting and fishing in the country."

Dawson is right. But he ignores the fact that for every Canadian rich and smart enough to invest in Canada there are 10 Americans equally rich and smart and twice as eager. Sheer weight of numbers may overwhelm us unless our governments step in. Present programs for developing recreational land, public and private, barely keep up with current demand. Much more foresight is needed. Ontario, conservationists say, will need three more Algonquin Parks within the next 10 years. The land for these parks should be bought now.

An obvious first move is to take a hard look at the tax-sale operations. Ontario MPP Leo Bernier, a Conservative backbencher, advocates a 90-day delay on the sale of tax lands to give the lands and forests department time to purchase the properties if it wishes. Broadcaster Larry Johnston suggests that public money to buy land going for taxes can easily be raised by levying higher licence fees on the American hunters and fishermen who use our recreational facilities. But Johnston, like other concerned outdoors experts, remains convinced that much more radical solutions must be considered: "We should lay down the principle that only Canadians can own land in this country. All nonresident property should be bought back by the government at its original purchase price. Canada is of value for what we have, not what we are. If we sell what we have, we're nothing."

Some of the problems — and ironies — such a policy of nationalization might involve are vividly illustrated by a situation now confronting the Nova Scotia government. A battle royal has developed in Cape Breton's Inverness County about the future of 1,900 acres of majestic shoreline at Cape Mabou. The province wants to acquire the land as part of a proposed national park. Most Cape Bretoners enthusiastically endorse the proposal. The limited commercialism that the park would permit could give an economic boost to the area.

However, the land is owned by a group of Americans dedicated to the idea that Cape Mabou's natural wilderness beauty should be preserved. Their leader is Mrs. Jean Rosner, a schoolteacher from Concord, Massachusetts, who has been buying abandoned farms in the area for 30 years and who now owns some 900 acres. She has been turning out mimeographed pamphlets pleading that Cape Mabou is in danger of being turned into another Disneyland. The government's moral dilemma: how to reconcile the interests of the natives with Mrs. Rosner's praiseworthy demands for conservation. Ultimately, Mrs. Rosner seems bound to lose.

The one consolation in the Cape Mabou situation is that Mrs. Rosner and her fellow Americans are not holding on to their properties simply because they want to make money. That, however, won't always be the case. Twenty years from now, if present trends continue, governments and private citizens who want to buy a piece of Canada will be going to somebody like Bill Wineberg, paying his price and liking it.

104 CANADIAN COMPANIES TAKEN OVER BY U.S. IN '70

Martin Dewey

Martin Dewey is a writer for the Toronto Daily Star.

Clary McMullen, 29, is a Grade 5 clerk with the Combines Investigations Branch of the Department of Consumer and Corporate Affairs in Ottawa.

At a salary range of $7,229 to $7,743 he has one of the most important jobs in Canada — the kind that in most other countries would be handled by an entire government agency.

But Clary McMullen remains totally unaware of his importance. So do his bosses. So, it seems, does everyone else in government.

His days are spent assembling and looking after a black loose-leaf book with a small white label identifying it as the Merger Register.

It contains the only official record anywhere in Canada of the day-by-day, month-by-month takeover of this country's industries by outsiders.

Only in that book do you learn that outsiders bought control of at least 117 Canadian business firms between January and mid-November of this year. That, characteristically 104 of these purchases were by Americans.

That there were another 76 takeovers in which the nationality of the acquiring firm, whether domestic or foreign, had not yet been discovered.

Only in that book do you learn, in short, that our industries are still subject to the most thoroughgoing takeover ever experienced by an advanced nation.

It confirms, moreover, that we are still in the midst of a high takeover trend which jumped from an average of 78 firms a year through most of the 1960s to 163 firms in 1968 and 168 in 1969.

It tells us that foreign investors, mainly American, are still energetically adding to holdings which already give them control of 8,500 Canadian firms at the very least and which have allowed them to dominate our manufacturing, extractive and resource-based industries.

Information of this kind is clearly of tremendous public importance at a time when all three political parties and the Canadian people as a whole have come to see our loss of economic sovereignty as one of the critical issues of our day. It's really the key to any enlightened response to the challenge of foreign investment.

This is clearly recognized in other countries, where major government ministries make it their business not only to keep track of foreign takeovers but to screen them first.

In Mexico, foreign investors who want to buy domestic industries have to apply to the ministry of trade and development as well as to the foreign affairs ministry.

Applications get a severe going over. They will be rejected outright if there is an intention to invest in prohibited industries in which foreigners are not allowed to own so much as a dollar's worth of stock. These include electrical generation and distribution, railroads, petroleum exploration and exploitation, insurance, finance and banking.

Minority holdings

Foreigners are also limited to minority holdings in a number of so-called restricted industries — petrochemicals, mining, publishing, broadcasting and general communications, and the showing of motion pictures.

Finally, foreigners wanting to buy or invest in a non-restricted industry are required to demonstrate to the two government ministries that the deal is in the national interest. Mexican authorities will want to know whether the investment will improve the country's export position, create jobs, introduce techniques or benefit a depressed area.

The policy works. Since 1937, when foreigners dominated Mexico's economy and owned its basic industries, a program of Mexicanization has reclaimed those industries and reduced foreign holdings to an overall minority in other areas.

Japan is even more finicky, and takeovers of domestic industries are banned outright. At best foreigners can own 20 per cent of an established Japanese firm and only 15 per cent of firms in restricted industries — most banking and finance, utilities, most domestic and overseas transportation, communications, mining and commercial fishing.

Takeovers screened

In France, takeover applications are screened by the foreign ministry and may be approved if they are deemed to be in the national interest. There are no rules and each case is examined on its own merits.

In general the French are not keen

on takeovers of existing companies and prefer foreign investors to establish new industries. Prospects of a foreign takeover are improved if it will create jobs, earn foreign exchange, assist in regional development or introduce new manufacturing techniques.

In Britain, foreign takeovers are screened by the Treasury and Board of Trade, which want to know how much new capital will be brought in and how the deal will affect exports and domestic trade.

But the rules are applied liberally and foreign ownership of British industry has passed 16 per cent, according to estimates, and is still climbing.

The British system leaves much to be desired, but it still ensures that all takeover bids are subject to government scrutiny. All we have in Canada is Clary McMullen and his black book, and even he is somewhat inaccessible.

The only way you can find out what is in the Merger Register is by going to Ottawa, making your way to his shared office on the 13th floor of a government building on Laurier Ave., and thumbing through it yourself.

If you can't manage this you must wait until the Combines Investigation Branch runs off the totals at the end of the year and publishes the results some three months later. No breakdowns by industry or by region. No dollar amounts. Just the number of firms taken over.

If more details are needed, you must be even more patient and await the pleasure of the government's slow and cumbersome reporting machinery.

Data six years old

The Dominion Bureau of Statistics does provide figures on the numbers of Canadian firms controlled in the United States, the United Kingdom and "other countries" —but its latest published information is six years old. A new report, expected in January, will bring us only to 1967.

If you want to know the dollar value of foreign acquisitions you can always turn to a DBS statement covering changes in amounts of direct foreign investment in Canada — but here the freshest information is for 1966, if anyone still cares.

Ironically, the only up-to-date information normally available to Canadians comes from the country we have most to worry about where foreign takeovers are concerned.

It is the Survey of Current Business published by the U.S. Department of Commerce which puts the latest price tag on acquisitions — telling us, for example, that U.S. investors spent $222 million on takeovers in Canada last year.

That's why Clary McMullen, Grade 5 clerk, is so important. His black book isn't very comprehensive when you come right down to it, and it is often sadly lacking in detail. But it is current. It is as vital and relevant as the graph at the foot of the hospital bed.

To open this book is to step into a world of writhing corporate octopuses with tentacles that sometimes get lost in the tangle and with appetites ranging from the gluttonous to the bizzare.

You learn, for example, that a heavy construction firm based in New York and known as Plaza Group Inc. has seen fit to absorb something called the Canadian Wig Company, address unknown to the Combines Branch.

You learn that no enterprise is too Canadian to be taken over. Adirondack-Sherwood Inc. of New Jersey buys out a manufacturer of hockey sticks in Sherbrooke, Quebec. Standard Brands, a Montreal-based U.S. subsidiary, swallows L. J. McGuinness of Toronto, Canada's last family-owned distillery.

No firm is too old

You learn that no firm is too old: We lose a sweater manufacturing concern in St. Catharines, established 1877. And no firm is too new: We lose the distribution arm of Cinepix of Montreal, a producer of feature films for our infant motion picture industry.

Nothing is too small: A maker of pipe nipples in Acton Vale, Quebec. And nothing is too big: A chain of dairies in Manitoba with 80 per cent of the market.

Nothing is too sensitive. Along with Ryerson Press and the textbook division of W. J. Gage Ltd., which account for a large chunk of the Canadian textbook market, we lose a distributor of newspapers and magazines in Windsor and theatre interests in the Maritimes.

Certainly nothing is secure. If a Toronto burglar bungles his work on premises protected by SIS Alarms Ltd., the alert now registers in a local alarm station owned by the William J. Burns Detective Agency of New York.

Fight in vain

And, no matter how hard we fight it, the end promises to be American for more and more of us. Two U.S. funeral parlor chains are just dying to bury us. Between them, Service Corporation International of Texas and International Funeral Services of Iowa have absorbed 34 funeral parlors across Canada in a two-year buying spree.

It's all there in Clary McMullen's black book, and the amazing thing is that it's there almost by accident.

The Merger Register is not designed as a record of takeovers. Its real function is to keep tabs on mergers and acquisitions in general and the fact that many of them are carried out by foreign companies is recorded simply in passing.

Equally amazing is the way this official government record is compiled. When it comes to major business activity, the Combines Investigations Branch is like the late American comedian Will Rogers: It only knows what it reads in the papers.

The idea is that everyone in Combines Investigations — 100 souls or so — is expected to circle any reference to mergers or acquisitions in the score or more newspapers, magazines and trade publications that circulate through the branch.

These circled references are pasted up by a librarian and passed along to Clary McMullen, who copies the information in a careful printed hand onto file cards. As each card reaches a steno the information is typed onto a loose-leaf sheet, and the Merger Register grows fatter by one page.

It's obviously not very scientific. Until the branch gets a chance to crosscheck its data with other government departments — much, much later — the register contains only what is disclosed in the news reports.

When a takeover involves a private Canadian company and a wholly owned subsidiary of a foreign company — which is allowed by Canadian law to masquerade as a private company — a page of the Merger Register will often carry only the names of the companies with the notation: No details.

Poignant little notes

Sometimes Clary McMullen will include a poignant little note such as "established 45 years" or "third-largest Canadian bus line." Such are the terse epitaphs for companies which were built on Canadian capital and Canadian enterprise and Canadian hopes and now belong to someone else.

Clary McMullen is doing his best, and so is the Combines Investigation Branch if you remember that take-overs aren't really their concern — or anyone else's.

Still, a visitor to that small office on Laurier Avenue can't help thinking that a black loose-leaf book full of newspaper clippings is a heck of a way to keep track of takeovers in the world's most taken-over country.

And he can't help thinking of the pen set on Clary McMullen's desk, with its two figurines depicting a voluptuous woman and a worried little fellow who is plainly out of his class. Printed underneath are the words: Mission Impossible.

Part 3

The Americans' massive involvement in our economy, and our relatively high standard of living which, to a degree, rests on that involvement, seem to resist any significant changes. Does American ownership threaten Canada's nationhood? If the answer is "yes," does that matter? If it matters, what can be done about it?

Should anything be done about American television, radio and magazines in Canada? If so, who is to do it?

POSITION PAPER ON U.S. INVESTMENT

It was a strange spectacle — hardly credible in any country but Canada — when Jean-Luc Pepin rose in the House of Commons recently to report on foreign control of our economy.

The minister of industry, trade and commerce was sorry he couldn't tell anyone how much of our economy is owned by outsiders at the moment, but he did have statistics drawn from 1967 tax returns. They showed that non-residents then controlled 56.7 per cent of our manufacturing, 82.6 per cent of our petroleum industry, 99.9 per cent of our oil refining and 60.6 per cent of our mining.

And that was that. If a chill fell over the House of Commons at these disclosures, it wasn't reported. If there were loud cries of dismay and outrage, we didn't hear about them. Mr. Pepin was allowed to catalogue the latest stage in the gradual economic demise of a nation as if he were reciting baseball scores.

Yes, a strange spectacle . . . on the government benches, something approaching detachment over the degree of foreign penetration of our economy. Outside Parliament, however, from one end of Canada to the other, we were seeing unmistakable stirring of new concern for this country of ours.

If we read it correctly, this concern is based on a dawning awareness that we are not just losing a business firm when a takeover occurs and not just losing an opportunity when outsiders initiate a new enterprise. What we are losing is sovereignty — economic, political and cultural.

The loss of economic sovereignty is self-evident. We didn't need the Dosco shutdown in Sydney, or the Dunlop shutdown here to drive home the point that millions of Canadian jobs hang on decisions taken in foreign boardrooms, or by foreigners in Canadian boardrooms.

We knew that, just as we know the decisions of foreigners are the key factor in determining levels of research in Canadian industry and our degree of economic sophistication, in shaping our patterns of saving, investment and consumption.

The loss of political sovereignty (or, more accurately, our failure to attain it after completing our long apprenticeship in the British Empire) is a much more subtle process.

Only occasionally do outsiders interfere directly in our affairs — as when Washington picks up the phone on behalf of U.S. business interests here (the Mercantile bank, Time Magazine and Reader's Digest), or

Reprinted with permission *Toronto Daily Star*, August 1, 1970.

when the U.S. treasury tells us how much foreign exchange we can hold.

Galling though such interventions may be, they remain the exception because it is in the nature of the new economic imperialism that the dominant power doesn't have to tell its dependency what to do; the dependency is a docile servant who has been taught to identify his well-being with that of his master.

It is here, in the area of things we don't do for fear of jeopardizing our second-hand affluence, that we discover a Canadian servitude which is massive and pervasive.

We don't reform our tax system; we daren't depart from the general U.S. model of relationships between government and business; we don't develop a distinctive foreign policy; we don't speak out against a war most Canadian detest, and we don't stop making weapons for that war.

We don't, in short, do anything that might conceivably make us appear to be fundamentally unreliable as a trading partner, as a country to make money in, as a military ally, or as a friend and companion in the ideological wars. Whatever our secret urgings, we don't offend.

We are infinitely accommodating, in fact, and we prove it by an apparently deliberate resolve to ensure that economic and political sovereignty is not alone as it gurgles down the drain. We toss in cultural sovereignty as well, making sure no Canadian child has to face life without Batman or a U.S. textbook in his school desk, or, when he gets older, an American professor at his university.

If he is ever in doubt what to think, we encourage access to his favorite U.S. newsmagazine, complete with a handy insert designed to help him flip his way superficially through Canadian affairs. And when he has a free moment from all this he can drive his American-designed car to an American drive-in movie and gorge himself on Coke and burgers from a U.S.-franchised hamburger chain.

The result has been what one would expect. In many critical areas of thought and activity, the U.S.-Canadian border has been all but obliterated. Throughout English-speaking Canada, and to a large extent in Quebec as well, the American way has in many vital respects become our way.

Yet the Trudeau government, in setting the objectives of Canadian foreign policy, not only failed to assign top priority to "safeguarding sovereignty and independence," but placed it in a secondary category of national aims — somewhere below economic growth, social justice and "quality of life."

However, the important thing — the overriding thing — is that the process of absorption is not yet complete. We haven't actually become Americans, in fact or in spirit, and the difference that remains between our two peoples has suddenly come to seem critical to many Canadians.

Broadly speaking, Canada has two choices:

1. To continue along present lines and eventually become a complete economic, political, social and cultural appendage of the United States without the benefits of full citizenship and no effective control over our future. We would have most of the disadvantages of being American citizens.

2. To attempt to steer an independent course on the assumption that if we can control our own destiny, we can build a better life as an independent people than we could hope to achieve as vassals of the United States.

What do we mean by a better life?

We mean a society which recognizes and respects the dignity of the individual and tries to make the economic system work for him instead of making him a mere cog in the productive machine.

We mean a society that values diversity above conformity.

We mean a society that rejects materialism as the be-all and end-all of life and emphasizes instead excellence in every form of human endeavor.

We mean a society that abhors violence and its causes, and stresses tolerance and human understanding.

We mean a society that is neither rampantly individualistic nor slavishly collective, but a sane balance between the two.

Economically, it would be a mixed society, with some public and some private ownership, depending on which was better suited to the job at hand. This pattern of ownership is already established in Canada and is in sharp contrast to the slavish worship of the free enterprise system in the United States.

Historically, our government has been more interventionist than in the United States. This role should continue and expand, with government acting to even up the balance between vested interests and the unorganized sections of society.

Even if we were completely free politically to follow this course, we would not have the economic means to achieve it unless Canadians owned more of the means of production. The lion's share of the wealth created by any society goes to the owners of the means of production, not to labor. To the degree that our economy is owned by foreigners, foreigners — not Canadians — will reap the maximum rewards.

Faced with these two broad choices, surely the best course for Canadians is to opt for a truly independent society in which we will be free to work out our own destiny. There is no assurance that we will succeed in all our objectives; but surely the challenge is worth the effort, especially when we consider the alternative.

As Canadians, we must find the courage to strike out on our own for the first time, in directions no one has charted for us. And at the top of our list of priorities, as the first and most urgent condition of survival, we must place the task of reclaiming our economic sovereignty. There is no other way.

At this point we must reject two opposite extremes of thinking among those who recognize foreign ownership as a problem. One is nationalization of foreign-owned enterprises; the other is the idea that it is too late for Canadians to "buy back" companies and industries already under foreign control.

Nationalization is urged by the Waffle group of the New Democratic Party on the ground that, since Canadian capitalists are no more enlightened than foreign capitalists, a transfer of ownership to their hands will do nothing to further needed economic and social change. This argument loses sight of the main point, which is that independence is necessary before the Canadian people can create the kind of economy and society they want. Also, if fair compensation were paid for the expropriated industries, nationalization would be terribly expensive, and might cripple development by cutting off access to two undoubted benefits of foreign investment: modern technology and managerial skills.

An "independent capitalist Canada" is preferable to a dependent capitalist Canada. We must first remove the American half-nelson on our economic development and restore the levers of control to this country if we wish at a second stage to opt out of "the American way of life."

Those who oppose any effort to "buy back" Canada through private investment claim the cost would be crippling, and that Canadians should concentrate instead on getting control of new industries with a promising growth potential. It's true the cost would be prohibitive if we tried to buy the industries back indiscriminately and over a short period of time. But the idea that we could get the new industries without buying into the old ones, is an illusion, because it is the old companies which spawn most of the new enterprises. For instance, it was Hudson's Bay Oil that wanted to take over Denison uranium mines. A very large part of new direct foreign investment comes from expansion of and takeovers by existing foreign-owned subsidiaries in Canada. Thus new investment and industries can proliferate without any opportunity for Canadian participation at all. It follows that a substantial amount of "buying back" will be necessary if Canadians are ever to gain control of the country's economic future.

There are two other important reasons for opening up the stock of foreign subsidiaries to Canadian buyers:

1. The entire internal accounting procedure — license fees, royalties, dividend payments, pricing of internal components — must then be altered (and scrutinized) in the interests of domestic stockholders and, by that very fact, in the Canadian interest. It is possible, for example, for American firms to evade the tax on their dividends sent home to the U.S. by labelling these as "royalties." This kind of evasion is much more

difficult when the company is not 100 per cent foreign-owned.

2. There's a shortage of blue-chip stocks in Canada for Canadian pension funds and mutual funds. The Canadian capital market is generally thin and weak and would benefit from the opening up of the shares of U.S. subsidiaries to Canadian investors. Otherwise, Canadian private capital will continue to be diverted to the United States.

The Star believes Canada should, as a general rule, aim at 51 per cent Canadian ownership of large companies in Canada. A law requiring this should take effect gradually — over 10 years, say — and should provide for exceptions or delayed application in the following cases:

(a) New developments in the resource field if suitable Canadian partners cannot be found; (b) Companies which are not making profits and may need more time before their shares are sold to the public; (c) Possibly companies in the automobile industry, such as General Motors. This industry is a near-monopoly, and government regulation rather than Canadian ownership appears to be the most practical way to supervise it in Canada's interests.

It's essential to have a plan for gradual Canadian participation in, and ultimate majority control of, most of the big foreign companies in Canada. But we must not suppose that this alone will solve the problems raised by foreign ownership. Buying back is a long-range proposition, since U.S. long-term investment alone is estimated at $40 billion. Our clear and obvious need is to assert some degree of control over the dominant foreign firms now, while there is still a Canadian identity to protect. The only way this can be done decisively is through government. Regulations calling for disclosure — now in the works at Ottawa — must be buttressed by measures which will make it possible for government to influence the decision-making process in the foreign-controlled sector before all the final decisions are taken.

The beginnings of an answer might lie in an investment control agency such as the federal government is reported to be considering. It should have two main tasks: To screen takeovers of Canadian companies and to "Canadianize" the functions of those firms which are already here and which dominate our economic life. Each of these tasks is so important and difficult as to require separate branches with their own staffs.

The function of the "Canadianizing" branch at first would be administer the corporate disclosure regulations and to enter into close, two-way consultative relationships with leading foreign firms. The agency would acquaint businessmen in the foreign sector with broad Canadian needs and encourage them to take these into account in laying their plans.

At a subsequent stage, the agency would be empowered to go beyond mere consultation and become something of a Canadian partner, able to influence decisions in the planning stages and, in extreme circumstances, to veto the decisions of foreign-controlled companies.

By these means the Canadian government could ensure that the foreign-controlled sector of our economy, far from being a threat to us, became an active and vigorous force in pursuit of Canadian purposes.

At the same time we would be going a long way toward solving the problems of bigness that J. K. Galbraith worries about: Firms so powerful they determine consumer wants,

distort resource allocation, control markets and set prices.

In "Canadianizing" the multi-national corporation, we would also be making it socially responsive. If we could pull it off, we would be the envy of the Western world.

The watchdog function of an investment control agency would be to assess proposed takeovers and movements of capital for their possible effect on the national interest. Each takeover bid should be judged on its economic merits, except where — as in the case of Denison Mines — the effect would be to shift the balance of control of an important industry from Canadians to outsiders. In such cases, and in all cases where no net economic benefit to Canada could be foreseen, takeovers should be blocked.

In approaching the specific problem of takeovers and direct foreign investment in general, we must recognize that it is already dangerously late in the day. A Star report three months ago concluded that some 7,000 Canadian firms are now controlled by Americans and that the number is growing by more than 300 a year. With the process moving this quickly, there is no time for leisurely solutions.

Another high priority is to launch a powerful Canada Development Corporation, with capital resources of at least $2 billion. Shares should be sold to the general public after the CDC has established itself, and an important part of its funding should come from pension funds, banks, insurance and trust companies.

The CDC should be particularly useful in correcting the structural defects that have been produced in the Canadian economy by our client-state relationship with the U.S.

The first of these defects flows from the fact that we have been to the more sophisticated economy of raw materials and natural resources to the more sophisticated economy our neighbors — the old business of being hewers of wood and drawers of water. The second is seen in what the Watkins task force called the "replica effect," in which our manufacturing sector has been developed as a small copy of the vast American manufacturing sector with little regard for economies of scale.

The Watkins report proposals for legislation to stop U.S. law from intruding into Canada offer a useful start. With U.S. anti-trust law blocked at the border, we will be able to encourage U.S. subsidiaries to merge or rationalize their efforts to fit the realities of our markets and exports needs.

If we are to eliminate the wasteful replica effect in the Canadian economy, we'll need bigness — not the kind of bigness that frightens people like Galbraith, but the responsible kind that becomes possible when government and the foreign giants start working together.

If we are to stop being hewers of wood and drawers of water, on the other hand, our great need will be capital — not the kind that comes into the country to own and control and exploit, but the kind that comes to participate and work alongside Canadian capital.

To achieve the right mixture of foreign and Canadian capital, we must marshal the vast private resources of this country — and this is where the Canada Development Corporation comes in.

The CDC should try to put new resource developments into Canadian hands, either by financing Canadian companies or by going into partnership with foreign investors.

The CDC should also encourage rapid development in the processing sector of our economy so that more and more semi-finished products could be made available for export and for our own use. The hewers of wood must start planning more lumber.

Here, as in other types of ventures, the CDC could proceed either by offering to finance Canadian-controlled enterprises or by taking on the role of entrepreneur and senior partner in inviting the participation of foreign capital.

Another major task of the CDC would be to underwrite new technologies in which Canadian firms showed special promise and to encourage independent Canadian development in certain of the important established technologies.

It's been suggested, for example, that the client-states of the future will be those which haven't developed their own computer industries. It would be up to the CDC to rescue us from this fate.

A basic part of any general plan should be to build up a category of protected industries in which foreign ownership is limited or excluded entirely. Successive governments have already made a useful start by insisting on Canadian control of banks and certain financial institutions, broadcasting outlets and now the uranium industry. The list can be lengthened as we go along, adding industries we want to protect because they are economically strategic (such as resource industries), because they are essential to our cultural independence (such as magazines and book distribution), or merely because we perceive an opportunity to develop them as dominantly Canadian enterprises (new technologies, a computer network, and so forth).

Also, there is no need to wait until Canadians can purchase control of foreign subsidiaries before injecting a strong Canadian presence in their boardrooms. Ottawa could require that within three years a majority of the directors of all large foreign-controlled firms in Canada shall be Canadian citizens living in Canada who are not full-time employees of the companies concerned.

To cover and maintain Canada's independence is a long-term project that will call for all the determination and persistence that Canadians and their governments can muster.

Foreign control of our economy has gone so far and is advancing so swiftly that a strong, many-sided program must be launched immediately to begin reversing the process. Canada, of course, still needs to import capital and should tell foreign investors they are welcome — if they accept the Canadian rules of the game. The rules proposed above would, we believe, preserve the independence of Canada for us and for our children.

WE MUST CULTIVATE OUR GARDEN

Stanley J. Randall

Stanley J. Randall was Ontario's Minister of Economics and Development from 1963-70.

Speech to the Rotary Club of Toronto, February 19, 1971.

What *is* the issue?

Stated as clearly as I can put it, I see the issue as a basic change in the average Canadian's view of his country as a full member in the broader world community.

What has happened is really quite simple. Over the past 20 years, we have grown up —grown up economically, politically, socially, and culturally. There are some people, of course, who say that Canada is still in many respects a boy who has passed his manhood, but is not yet a man. There's still talk of our being hewers of wood and drawers of water. And we're trying to get rid of that image.

In any event, Canadians cut the umbilical cord that tied us to the old British Empire. And the Commonwealth, I think, has never really provided the same kind of emotional security that Canadians enjoyed as a member of the empire that spanned the globe.

Remember, when you were a kid, how the maps colored British possessions in red — and when red held

Reprinted with permission of the Honourable Stanley J. Randall, Minister of Trade and Development.

no sinister political shadings? Remember how it was kind of comforting to know we were part of that all-encompassing world?

But cut adrift from the Mother Country, we soon found a substitute comfort in closer relations with the United States. *We began to be increasingly aware of being North Americans in the continental sense without being Americans in the national sense.* And it wasn't chance that brought us into military alliances with the U.S. We entered agreements, when it became obvious that Britain could no longer guarantee our national security. As an extra bonus, the emergence of continentalism in the war and post-war years paid off in economic terms.

As long as the U.S. was looked on as the leader of the free world, as long as there was a polarization of power between two blocs, Canada's position as a friend of the United States was never seriously questioned. Given this situation, U.S. investment was regarded as a positive economic benefit, and the political problems could be conveniently forgotten. In fact, our viewpoint was: If Canada and the U.S. can't create mutual political institutions that will allow man to survive in the nuclear age, then which nations can?

But for 10 years now, this idyllic picture of the world has been shattered by one event after another. I'll list only a few: The formation and success of the EEC . . . the stagnation of Britain under socialism and Britain's decline as a world power . . . the fragmentation of the communist camp . . . the emergence of Japan . . . the continuing crises in the Middle East . . . the tragedy of South East Asia . . . the internal unrest in the United States (though *Time* magazine's cover story this week is called "The Cooling of America").

And these events were paralleled by changes taking place in Canada — culminating in two terrorist kidnappings, the murder of one of the victims, threats of insurrection and assassination, and rumors of revolution.

Canada's Centennial and Expo 67 gave us pride and confidence. But many events of 1970 certainly removed our complacency . . . removed our it-can't-happen-here attitude.

The challenge now is to recover our wisdom, restraint, and openness . . . to recover our vision of greatness. And radical nationalists aren't helping at all with their negative, narrow, and noisy pessimism.

It's always convenient for the radical to ignore history. Canadian economic nationalists do it like (broken) clockwork. In fact, it's been pointed out that the economic nationalist version of history sounds like a stuck record — the voices change, but the refrain is the same: French-English relations are in crisis, and Canada is a colony dominated by Great Britain or the United States — or both.

To keep their griping up to date, they should also direct their invective towards the huge Michelin Tire Company in the Maritimes and towards the Japanese investment in our energy resources in the West — and at two more areas of Canada that can't afford the wrath or luxury of economic nationalism.

But politicians ignore reality and history at their peril — the record is there to haunt them in the future. For example: The present problem of foreign involvement in Canada's economy didn't just grow like Topsy. It's been with us for a long time. And it's something Canadians encouraged through our federal policies.

The basic philosophy underlying Canadian economic and commercial policy for the past 25 years has been to ensure that Canada attracted foreign investment. For example:

— we kept our tax system in line with that of the U.S., our major trading partner.

— we entered into tax agreements with foreign countries to ensure that profits on foreign investments weren't taxed twice. (And if we buy some of the proposals in Mr. Benson's White Paper, we'll run into trouble here.)

— we operated a monetary policy to keep interest rates in Canada marginally higher than in the U.S.

— we maintained a protective tariff that encouraged foreign companies to set up branch plants in the Canadian market.

— we asked for, and received, special treatment from U.S. law that restricted U.S. investment in other countries.

— we negotiated special deals with the U.S. on a wide number of products — not the least of which was the auto pact, which created 20,000 new jobs for Canadians. And the auto pact also created, in effect, a type of common market for autos and auto parts. It has solidly worked to our benefit. And it's the same kind of trade deal worked out by European countries in forming a common market. And no country in that trading bloc, incidentally, has lost its sovereignty.

Now, Canadian nationalists have argued that we no longer need foreign capital, and that Canadian money is being used to finance a so-called U.S. take-over. But why shouldn't a U.S. subsidiary in Canada try to suceed, try to expand, try to create jobs? And would the nationalists be any happier if this expansion was financed by the importation of more money?

The fact remains that Canada has been, year in and year out, a net importer of capital on top of the savings we generated ourselves. And we have used that capital to develop our economy, to build roads, to construct schools and hospitals, and to create jobs. Only in exceptional cases has Canada been a net exporter of capital.

In fact, I foresee — as do others — a future in which Canadians will invest more in other countries than foreigners invest here. I foresee an era in which countless Canadian-bred multinational firms will do business around the world. To interfere with our money going out in investment — or with investment coming into Canada — would be to stand in the way of our future growth.

I'm not going to argue at this time whether Canadians have used foreign capital as wisely as we should have. As I've often said, *the closest to perfection a person ever comes is when he fills out a job application form.*

But the central fact remains that the impact of immigration over the past 20 years ruled out any possibility of financing our growth out of our own savings. You can't have one of the fastest-growing populations and labor forces in the western world and raise the necessary capital from domestic sources. It simply can't be done — not if you want to give people a rising standard of living at the same time you have a rapidly rising labor force.

In the last 20 years, over 1½ million persons have come to Ontario, the "province of opportunity." It's not the "province of opportunity" by accident. It takes a heap of working to make a province a "province of opportunity." It takes a lot of motivation and morale. Ontario's gross provincial product, for example, grew from $17 billion in 1963, when I became Minister of Trade and Development, to an expected $37.6 billion this year. That's more than double!

And that's what it boils down to! We have grown at a very fast rate in terms of population, resource development, social services, industrial base, transportation, and communication. We've emerged as a predominantly industrial society, because we've concentrated on it.

I'm aware that Canada's development has been uneven. Along with hard work, Ontario has been fortunate to have been the leader. But we have, as a country, undergone a transformation without undue cost to any group or class in Canada — indeed, the majority of Canadians have benefited. The people of Quebec and the Maritimes — and to a lesser extent, the western farmers — do feel left out. Certainly the job ahead is to get the industrial system spread throughout Canada, so that everybody can share in its benefits.

But — and this is a big *but* — we won't be able to do this without help. As Prime Minister Trudeau said recently — *and it's one of the few things he's said recently that I can quote in public* — it's one thing for hot-house intellectuals to talk about the threat of foreign take-over, when their jobs aren't on the line . . . It's another thing when an unemployed worker is told there's no job, because we won't let a firm into his town, simply because it's *foreign owned or controlled.*

These self-styled intellectuals are persons whose education and intelligence are seldom on speaking terms. They usually take more words than necessary to tell more than they know. And here's where they and I ultimately part company!

For these economic illiterates are willing to reject the realities of a competitive world, even if it costs somebody his livelihood, his pride, and his dignity — not to mention his contribution to our economy. *When jobs are on the line, I'm ready to go a long, long way to accommodate anyone who has a legitimate interest in creating jobs and incomes for Canadians — anywhere in this country.*

* * *

I'm a Canadian. I'm an Ontarian. I love this country. There's no place else I'd rather be. This is where I took my stand, and this is where I grew. And many people who choose Ontario as their home come here to get away from the restrictions on human liberty and opportunity imposed in socialist countries. They come to Ontario, because they recognize the chance to better their lives and the lives of their families.

I don't want to see a Canada devoid of the pulse of international business and competition. A strong and dynamic business environment keeps high-caliber people working in Canada — the kind of people who generate jobs for other people.

For over 100 years, Canadians have lived in one of the most open societies known. And I doubt they would be willing to give up their liberty to do business throughout the world or to stop the world from doing business here.

One of the reasons I went into politics was the challenge. I think that the clash of viewpoints in the political arena is necessary to find the best way of governing this country. I'm also an unrepentant free enterpriser. *I believe that what this country needs is less emphasis on free . . . and more on enterprise!* I believe that competition in a free market is beneficial both to the consumer and to the competing industries.

That's why the U.S. economy is the most dynamic in the world. We may not like some of the policies of the U.S., but they are the model for the whole world when it comes to the production and distribution of the products of industry . . . and that's what creates jobs.

It's been constructively recommended that Canada's nationalist socialists spend as much time studying Servan-Schreiber as they do spouting their current French favorite, Franz Fanon. They might learn that you don't need to be anti-Canadian to be pro-foreign. *But the sort of nationalist I have in mind is a guy whose opinions always manage to keep up with yesterday. And he always knows what his opinion will be tomorrow.*

It's easy for the socialists to say: "The U.S. is bad. U.S. business is bad. And therefore U.S. corporations are doubly bad." It's easy for Joe Greene to change his colors again and talk about "the sudden and tragic disappearance of the American dream." We Canadians appear to be having a few nightmares of our own lately.

What's so bad about American companies in Canada? What have they done that's against the law? And if we don't like the laws governing foreign corporations in Canada, we can change them! So what is it that makes some Canadians so afraid of them? Is it at all possible that the economic nationalist is envious? Is he afraid of the competition? Is he frightened he can't compete with the giants of the U.S. industry?

* * *

In my many years in private business and in my eight years as Ontario's Minister of Trade and Development, I've reached a definite conclusion about Canadian businessmen. Given an even break, they can compete with anyone! They can produce quantity and quality. They can sell at competitive prices and back it up with delivery and service. They've proven they can be productive and efficient, competing successfully despite protective tariffs, quotas, and other restrictions . . .

CAPTAIN CANADA OF 1971

Walter Stewart

Canada has recently witnessed the blossoming of two new brands of nationalism; both are aimed at loosening the American grip on our economy, but there their resemblance ends. They are the nationalisms of left and centre, of socialism and free enterprise, of radical upheaval and moderate change — in short, the nationalisms of Melville Watkins and Joe Greene. Some day soon Canadians will have to choose one of these brands — or some minor variation of either — or, not choosing, slide unresisting into a continental embrace. Before we make that choice, we should know something about these nationalisms, where they come from, where they lead, and the men behind them.

Melville Watkins is an economist, a professor at the University of Toronto, a national vice-president of the NDP, and the spiritual leader of the Waffle, the harrying force on the left wing of that party. He is expected to be the Waffle candidate for the NDP leadership next April. If he runs, he won't win, but he will make a respectable enough showing to jolt the staider elements of the party. He is a slender man of medium height and unprepossessing appearance. With his prominent nose, slightly buck teeth and unambitious chin, he looks a little like a chipmunk with a PhD. He wears glasses and a donnish expression, so that despite the long hair and Mod clothes that tend to link him to the young radicals who are his chief followers, he is in no danger of being mistaken for a hippie. When he speaks, his strongest gesture is an outward stroking of both hands near shoulder level, as if he were smoothing out somebody's chest-high bedspread. When he laughs, his head goes back, his face cracks and he produces a sound somewhere between a giggle and a whinny. Unfailingly clever, uncommonly courteous, he speaks a clear, crisp prose that is as rare from the front of a political platform as from the back of an economics lectern. (There is never any doubt about what he says, or where he stands. After one long argument, I burst out, "You're a bloody revolutionary! You want to smash everything and start again!" "That's right," he said.) He never harangues an audience, never speaks down to it, always informs and seldom stirs it. Despite a deluge of recent publicity, he is utterly without pretension. "I hate the cult of leadership," he says, and means it. Within the Waffle, he is treated as one voice, and one vote, no more. At heart, he is a Populist.

Joe Greene is a lawyer, a Liberal

Reprinted with permission of Walter Stewart, in *Maclean's*, November 1970.

politician, and federal Minister of Energy, Mines and Resources. Hard-driving and ambitious, he has tried twice for the provincial and once for the federal leadership of his party. He is a lanky hank of a man, over six feet tall, with striking features — deep-set hazel eyes, a thrusting nose, a jutting chin — topped by a becoming mop of silver hair. He is an orator in the old style, with quips and cracks and giant gestures. When he speaks, his head thrusts forward like an angry eagle, and his hands bank and wheel through the air before diving behind his back to take up positions at the top of his hips, while he leans into his favorite political role — the Ottawa Valley Abe Lincoln. He seldom tells an audience anything it doesn't already know, and seldom fails to stir it. He, too, is an attractive politician, known for his jokes (shortly after he was named Minister of Agriculture, he informed a Vancouver audience, "When they told me I was coming west to see the golden nematode [a plant pest], I thought it was a Victoria nightclub"), his toughness (when a farms spokesman tried to heckle him during an Ottawa meeting, Greene simply shouted him into silence. "Don't try to bull-roar me," he thundered, "I've seen your kind before") and his flexibility (last December, he spoke approvingly of a "continental approach" to energy resources; this April, when a reporter asked him about the phrase, he said, "I don't think there is any such animal. It is a term used by journalists." A high-ranking civil servant commented, "He has that marvelous capacity for shedding what has gone before and going on to the next thing"). He is popular with the general public, who find him folksy, not quite so popular with his cabinet colleagues, who find him foxy. "I'm damned if I know what the real

Joe Greene is like," one of them said. "He's been acting so long, I doubt if he knows himself."

Greene and Watkins agree that the U.S. owns and controls too much of the Canadian economy, and that the time has come to assert our nationality, but their approaches to this common problem are drastically different.

Watkins argues that the U.S. has come to control so much of Canada because we are a sister and weaker capitalist state. Capitalism is by nature aggressive and international. The multinational corporations that are its modern expression simply flow across borders to take what they want. As it happens, most of those corporations are American, and much of what they want is in Canada, and so we find ourselves increasingly taken over. But Watkins argues that this intrusion is only part of the real problem, which is the failure of capitalism. Despite decades of a so-called Welfare State, many Canadians still live in grinding poverty because the free enterprise system does not work, and cannot be made to work except for a few people at the top. The answer is to set up a democratic socialist state, whose independence would be assured through national planning of investment and the public ownership of the means of production. Bringing power and prosperity to ordinary people is the first concern, and that can only be done through socialism. If he had to choose between socialism and nationalism, Watkins would choose socialism, but he thinks the two are inseparable. Canada cannot be independent unless socialist, cannot be socialist unless independent.

Greene wasn't at all sure, until a few months ago, that it mattered who owned what in Canada. We needed U.S. capital. In fact, our prosperity had been built on it, and that meant selling control over large sectors of our economy. As long as we agreed, essentially, with U.S. aims, no harm was done. "Our only complaint was that we weren't more like the Americans, that we didn't make as much money as they did." But then the American dream went sour, in the jungles of Asia and along the hot, black pavements of U.S. cities, and Canadians began to want something else, a society less dollar-driven than the American one. Then, and only then, did the issue of foreign ownership become important, in Greene's view. If we want to build a distinctive society, it cannot be done by aping our neighbors; instead, we must take the best of what they have to offer and combine it with the Canadian traits of common sense and compromise into a new way of life. To do that, we must win back control of our economy, by beating the Americans at their own game. We must develop our own international corporations, raise our own capital, write our own rules for economic and cultural control, and make them stick. The tools are plainly visible — the Canada Development Corporation, the Canadian Radio-Television Commission, a new foreign policy — we have only to make them work.

Watkins' objection to the Greene approach is that it is spineless and futile; capitalism cannot cure our national *malaise*. Greene's objection to the Watkins approach is that it is unnecessary and unworkable; socialism is a cure worse than the disease.

Why do two intelligent, informed Canadians disagree so drastically? In a word, background.

Melville Watkins was born on May 15, 1932, on a farm just outside the small town of McKellar, near Parry Sound, Ontario. He and a twin brother (now a federal civil servant) were the second and third in a family of six born to a laborer. Watkins attended a two-room public school in McKellar and a high school in Parry Sound. In the summers, he worked as a bellhop in a tourist hotel, where fat, unpleasant Americans gave him fat, pleasant tips. A favorite pastime was to give U.S. tourists faulty road directions, so they would get lost. It was only a joke, but reflected real bitterness. In Watkins' world, somebody else — and the Americans were just a symbol of this — was always in charge. Somebody else called the shots for his family and his community. It didn't seem right. The town went down during the Depression, came back up during the war, when a factory opened, went back down again when the war ended and the factory closed. None of it had anything to do with the local people; they didn't make decisions, they suffered them. "To grow up in such a community, you begin to sense at an early age where the power lies and where it doesn't. A feeling of powerlessness hangs over you like smog."

A brilliant student, Watkins finished high school at 16, went on to the University of Toronto, and has been absorbed in academic life ever since. He did postgraduate work at the Massachusetts Institute of Technology, met and married a Boston-area girl ("She's utterly apolitical") and joined the Democratic left as a supporter of Adlai Stevenson and an opponent, if anything, of Canadian nationalism, which seemed petty and binding. It was only after his return to Toronto as an economics professor that Watkins became radicalized. In the early 1960s, everything began to happen at once — Vietnam, Black Power, student unrest, American encroachment — and everything seemed linked to a theme that stretched back to McKel-

lar, the tug-of-war between a few people who had power and many who lacked it. Watkins knew where he stood on that issue, and the more he became involved, the more he moved to the left, the more he came to regard the U.S. as an imperialist state, which must not be allowed to despoil Canada.

In 1966, writing in the *Canadian Forum,* Watkins had some kind things to say about Walter Gordon's book *A Choice For Canada.* That review, coupled with his own growing academic reputation, led to his appointment to Gordon's commission of inquiry into foreign ownership and the structure of Canadian industry. The result was the *Watkins Report,* which contained enough compromises to win the supporting signatures of economists as diverse in their views as Abraham Rotstein and A. E. Safarian but did not go nearly far enough to satisfy Watkins. It tinkered with various measures to meet American control, but evaded what seemed to him to be the obvious solution: socialism. Even so, it was brushed off by the Canadian government, and Walter Gordon, who had fought for the report, left active politics.

The disgruntled economist took his cause into the ranks of the NDP, where he soon discovered that socialism was almost as unwelcome a term as it had been among Liberals. Undaunted, he determined to thrust the NDP leftward, and he has been working hard at that task ever since, with the Waffle, a loose grouping of Leftists who took the title as an ironical comment on the rest of the party. (The name first appeared in writing in the letters of union organizer Giles Endicott, who signed himself The Waffle King.) In a sense, Watkins is still trying to do what couldn't be done in McKellar — to wrest power down to ordinary people, and to give the Americans a bum steer.

Joe Greene has nothing so drastic in mind. "The Americans are our friends," he says. He says it often. In fact, during the famous speech in Denver, Colorado, in which he staked out his nationalist position, he boosted Canadian-American friendship 15 times and said, nine times, that whatever Canadian nationalism was, it was not anti-American. Whatever Joe Greene is, he is not anti-American. In fact, it is a little difficult to make out just *what* he is.

It is somehow typical of the man that his name is not Joe but John James (Joe was a high-school nickname that stuck), and that, despite his platform role as an Arnprior hayseed, he is a city slicker from Toronto. His father was a mining engineer who turned stockbroker, a job he still holds at the age of 81. Greene was born on June 24, 1920, in north Toronto, went to University of Toronto Schools, and first remembers Americans as a distinct group from watching baseball at Maple Leaf Stadium. "They were always the best ballplayers." After high school, he worked for a printing firm and a mining company before joining the Air Force and going overseas to win a DFC as an observer with a night-fighter squadron. After the war, he completed his education at the University of Toronto and Osgoode Hall Law School, then moved to Arnprior, the hometown of the girl he married during his college years. As one of only two lawyers in town — the other, his law partner, was a Tory — Greene naturally gravitated into politics and won a seat on the Arnprior council.

He ran into trouble when he and his partner, acting for a development company, neglected to tell people about that link when they supported a bylaw granting the company special concessions. "Everybody knew about it anyway," says Greene. Investigators from the Ontario Department of Municipal Affairs were not so charitable; they referred to "a melee of illegality and irregularity" and branded the performance of the two lawyer-councillors "improper." However, no action was taken — Greene said later, "I'm just damn glad I learned my lesson before coming to Ottawa" — and the incident did not hurt him either in his unsuccessful bid for the Ontario Liberal leadership in 1958 or his successful run for a federal seat in 1963.

The new MP for Renfrew South made an immediate impact on Ottawa with a maiden speech blasting the facilities available to MPs, and the fact that they had to share cubbyhole offices with their secretaries. (Since his elevation to the cabinet, Greene has certainly improved his own amenities; refurbishing his executive office cost the taxpayer $15,635.20. Ordinary MPs are still sharing cubbyholes.) The speech showed that Greene was no run-of-the-mill backbencher, but there was no room for him on the front benches. He became bored, and ran again for the provincial leadership, in 1964. He didn't win — despite a vigorous campaign in which he charged the provincial Attorney General with, of all things, conflict of interest — but he ran well enough to make his appointment to the federal cabinet in 1965 a logical step. He was given the agriculture portfolio, partly because there were no western Liberal MPs, partly because he had cultivated a rural image that went down well. He worked hard at that rural image, even to the extent of denying his own considerable learning. When Douglas Fisher of the NDP uncorked an attack on him, Greene drawled, "Some of Mr. Fisher's classical allusions evaded me. If they were Biblical they would be much clearer, because in the Ottawa Valley ours is a humble form of learning."

If he was not a brilliant success as agriculture minister, he sounded like one. "If words could move wheat," harrumphed Dalton Camp, "Joe Greene would have sent it to the moon." He was the best orator the Liberals had, and it was his platform style — Abe Lincoln with just a touch of John F. Kennedy — that won him a respectable 169 votes on the first ballot in the 1968 federal leadership race and a spot in Prime Minister Trudeau's new cabinet. For the 1968 election, Greene left Arnprior, where redistribution had made his riding a dubious battleground, and fled to the safety of Niagara Falls, which had been Liberal since the seat was formed. It was a prudent rather than a popular move. "As soon as the going got tough," an Arnprior editor complained, "he got out." It turned out to be unnecessary, too — a Liberal won the seat, after all — but Greene has no regrets. "I don't want to stay in one place all my life," he said. "I regard every move as a challenge."

He had barely settled into his new portfolio, Energy, Mines and Resources, when he suffered two severe heart attacks — in November, 1968, and January, 1969 — and he spent several months recuperating. (Otto Lang minded the store as acting minister.) Back at work in mid-1969, Greene made headlines toward the end of the year by apparently embracing a policy of continental resource-use after a Washington conference with U.S. Secretary of the Interior Walter Hickel. Canadian reaction was sharply unfavorable and, early this year, the word was around Ottawa that Greene was headed for the sidelines in the next cabinet shuffle.

Then came the speech to the Independent Petroleum Association of America in Denver, on May 12, with its clear statement of Canadian nationalism — "Canadians are determined that they will build something which is clearly their own, and not the pale and small image of the great and powerful civilization to our south" — and a flat rejection of the American example — "I will say to you that, yes, a part of the cause for the rise of that new Canadian nationalism and determination to build something unique rests in the *malaise* that exists in your land — what appears to many as the sudden and tragic disappearance of the American dream, which, in some ways, has turned to nightmare."

It has been suggested that Greene's Denver speech was basically a ploy designed to protect his cabinet position, but he flatly rejects the notion. "I had been through two heart attacks," he said. "My heart had stopped twice. You don't come out of that and say, 'I'm going to secure my position in the cabinet.' When I have made whatever small contribution I am able to, I will be glad to pass the baton to someone else."

The speech was a response, he said, to an upwelling of Canadian nationalism, a heart cry that somehow missed his acute political antennae in late 1969, but came through loud and clear a few months later. "I had not been concerned with American control because Canadians seemed to put jobs and economic opportunities first. Now they were saying, 'No, there is something more to life than chasing a buck.' They wanted to build something new, and they were willing to pay the price. A politician is a pragmatist; if we have some talent, it is in the ability to sense these things and act on them. That is what I did."

In short, his nationalism is of the follow-in-front variety, designed to reflect rather than create a Canadian mood. Since Denver, the energy minister has paddled back to midstream with all deliberate speed, and in one recent speech on oil development, he sounded an almost continental note. His nationalism is not anti-American — for Greene has always looked up to Americans — not anti-capitalist — for capitalism has served him well — and as different from the nationalism of Melville Watkins as it can be.

Of these two nationalisms — one deep-rooted, rationalized in economic theory and dogmatized in political philosophy, the other late-blooming, pragmatic and flexible — the Greene variety seems more likely to win wide acceptance.

After all, Watkins asks us to meet the American challenge by tearing our society down, rooting out capitalism, and building again; in fact, he says there is no point in doing anything less. He admits that the much milder medicine prescribed by Walter Gordon in his 1963 budget proved too strong for most Canadians, but thinks a new generation will and must accept his stronger purgative some day. "Radical solutions always look improbable," he says, "but nothing else seems to work."

If we follow Greene — or lead him — there is nothing, really, we must do. It is all being looked after. The CDC will find native capital, the CRTC will safeguard native culture, and the occasional tough speech to American oil barons will ease the pressure. All we have to do is to keep the cards and letters coming. His solution to our national dilemma is less than drastic. Whether it is a real solution, only time will tell.

JUNEAU'S REVOLUTION: MAKING TV HISTORY

Robert Fulford

For decades everyone had been saying that the Canadian broadcasting system should be Canadian. Sir John Aird, the head of the first royal commission on broadcasting, said it in 1929. The Massey Commission said it in 1951. The Fowler Commission said it in 1957. Every parliamentary committee that so much as glanced at the situation said it, again and again. And yet through all those years the Canadian broadcasting system grew more and more American. The CBC may have been dominated by Canadian programmes in the radio days, but when TV came along, its English-language network nearly drowned in Hollywood-produced programmes on film. The private TV stations, for their part, made little more than a few gestures toward Canadian programming, and the private radio stations hardly did that.

And then, on February 12, 1970, the Canadian Radio-Television Commission announced that this period was at an end. It proposed that in the future both the CBC and the private TV stations be forced to devote sixty per cent of their prime evening time to Canadian programmes; and that radio stations, for their part, be re-

quired to devote thirty per cent of their time to Canadian music.

The chairman of the commission, Pierre Juneau — who with this announcement obviously became the most important single figure in Canadian mass culture — said that the CRTC would consider criticism of this proposal. It would listen to argument; the proposals were not "rigid"; but they were "firm."

The implications were enormous. Juneau was saying that he planned to order various Canadian institutions to do what everyone had always said they should do. It was as if a government body dealing with air pollution had actually told the private industries of Canada to stop polluting the air; or as if some federal authority were to say that the auto makers had to figure out some way to make safe cars, whether they felt like it or not. Juneau was suggesting no less than this: that what we had all said *should* be done actually *could* be done and *would* be done.

Now, some very good arguments can be made against Juneau and his proposals; and, considering his newly increased importance, perhaps these

Reprinted with permission of *Saturday Night*, May 1970.

arguments should be stated, as bluntly as possible. For instance:

(1) Juneau doesn't seem to understand the importance of commercials in Canadian broadcasting. He doesn't seem to grasp the point that advertising is what television and radio are about. Perhaps this is a result of his background, which was essentially in the National Film Board. The NFB depends on subsidy, not sales, so Juneau perhaps has never had to deal with the realities of advertising.

(2) Juneau apparently doesn't understand that the public is very, very stupid. This, too, may result from his Film Board career — the NFB, notoriously, has made films for people who like good films. It may also be a product of Juneau's aristocratic French-Canadian origins. He seems to believe, if one can judge by his comments, that in the absence of contrary evidence people should be treated as if they were intelligent.

(3) Juneau doesn't know that English-speaking Canadians won't watch Canadian programmes. This, too, may be a result of his French-Canadian background. For the last few years it has been the law in Canada that TV stations must devote at least fifty-five per cent of their broadcasting time to "Canadian content." In English-speaking Canada, most of the stations have provided this much and no more. But in French Canada the stations have averaged sixty to seventy per cent, voluntarily. This may have given Juneau a mistaken idea that Canadians as a whole want to watch other Canadians talking, singing and telling jokes.

(4) Juneau apparently doesn't know that Canadians can't write songs and make records. The idea of playing Canadian music was thus received by some commercial radio stations with dismay. How could anyone be so wrong?

In all these ways Juneau violated the conventional wisdom of Canadian culture. In his happy ignorance he (along with his fellow commissioners) took an approach that must certainly revolutionize Canadian broadcasting. And of course the fact is that Juneau's ignorance is not ignorance but freshness. He has brushed aside what "everybody knows" and decided to find out what actually can be done. In the process he has forced broadcasters and many others to re-assess their relationship to Canada and the Canadian future.

Some of us felt, in the 1950s and the early 1960s, that the whole idea of Canadian content, measured by percentages, was pretty silly.

One good Canadian programme, we argued, would probably be worth more than six bad ones; so why measure in hours? We knew — those of us, at least, who followed rather uneasily the deliberations of the Board of Broadcast Governors — that those administering the system had shown no real evidence of knowing the difference between good and bad in broadcasting. Indeed, they seldom indicated that they cared how the broadcasters filled their quota, so long as the percentages came out right.

And indeed, the harshest critics of the BBG's Canadian content policy were proved correct. The private TV stations provided Canadian content, all right, but as those critics predicted it was usually the worst sort of junk. Cheap talk shows and game shows, for instance, usually shoved into the hours with the smallest audiences. The BBG, in ruling broadcasting from 1958 to 1968, was in no position to encourage a better situation. At its head were amateurs of broadcasting who knew little about programming and believed that when they announced percentage goals their most serious work was done.

The CRTC is in a radically different situation. The commission itself is manned partly by experienced broadcasters; moreover, it has hired some of the best broadcasters Canada has produced — Sydney Newman, the drama producer, is the most distinguished of them — as advisers and consultants. Since it began to operate it has looked deeply into every aspect of broadcasting, from finance to programming. When the CRTC meets a broadcaster it meets him on terms of professional equality. It offers not empty rhetoric but opinions based on detailed facts.

Thus its decision to demand more Canadian programmes in prime time comes out of a study of the details of broadcasting in various parts of this country. The CRTC of course knows what every Canadian set owner knows: that our broadcasting stations are heavily Americanized. But it also believes it knows something else: that things don't have to be this way, that when you study the economics you discover that the stations, on demand, can perform much better.

The proposal to force broadcasters to schedule Canadian programmes in prime time was answered by some of them — the head of CTV, for instance — with the warning that this might mean a dilution of quality. It seems to me to be calculated to produce the opposite effect. If Canadian programmes must be seen when audiences are at their greatest — and thus the potential of commercial revenue at its highest — then broadcasters will be much more likely to provide programmes of quality.

The announcement of the new proposals in February came as a shock to many people both inside and outside broadcasting. It shouldn't have. Since Juneau and his fellow commissioners began making their first decisions, more than a year ago, they have been demonstrating that they take their work much more seriously than most regulatory agencies.

When they cancelled one small station's license for failing to provide a service to the community, they began to hint at what was to come. After all, the Federal Communications Commission in the United States, in the course of some four decades, had never seen fit to take such an obvious step.

But when they announced their policy on cable TV they began to make broadcasting history. Cable TV, the CRTC told us, was not to have a free ride on the back of broadcasting. Cable operators were expected to create their own programmes and put back into their communities some of the money they were taking out. Immediately the commissioners changed the status of cable TV from yet another license-to-print-money (in Lord Thomson's famous phrase) to the status of a public utility with public responsibilities. About the same time, the CRTC began to make it clear that it believed broadcasting stations should be owned in their communities and should reflect the needs of their communities.

None of this, it was obvious from the beginning, would come easily. Juneau and the others had set out, clearly, to change the face of broadcasting in Canada. To change it from American-dominated to Canadian-dominated. To convert its private sector from irresponsibility to responsibility. To make it not simply a reflection of whatever social and com-

94

mercial winds blow in the country but a creative contributor to Canada as a whole.

The commissioners must have known from the beginning they were attempting something close to the impossible. In a field demoralized on the one hand by a gone-to-seed public corporation, and corrupted on the other by the deadest sort of commercialism, they were calling for hope, optimism, and national ambition on the grand scale. In the middle of a dull, anxious winter, the February announcements of the Canadian Radio-Television Commission were a remarkable sign of life. The idea of Canadian broadcasting, it turned out, wasn't dead yet.

STATEMENT OF PURPOSE

Committee for an Independent Canada

We believe that Canadians today share a surging mood of self-awareness. But this mood must be translated into effective policies, or we may risk the erosion of Canadian independence by default. Government guidelines and vague political promises are no longer enough.

The Committee for an Independent Canada has been established to speak out with one strong voice for the survival of this country. It represents men and women from every corner of Canada, of all ages, professions and political hues, who believe that meaningful independence can only be secured by an active process that involves the day-to-day participation of concerned citizens which will lead to government action.

We realize the benefits that Canada derives from being part of the western hemisphere and we do not want to close this country to the foreign capital which it may need. But our land won't be ours much longer if we allow it to continue to be sold out to foreign owners. Not if we allow another culture to dominate our information media.

If we are to ensure this country's survival, our governments must adopt legislative policies that will significantly diminish the influence presently exerted by outside powers — their citizens, their corporations and their institutions — on Canadian life. We believe that the federal parliament together with provincial legislatures in relevant areas of their jurisdiction, must take urgent measures in the following areas:

1. The present level of foreign ownership of the economy is unsatisfactory for Canadians since major decisions affecting our economic

life are taken outside this country. We urge the Government to implement policies designed to increase the proportion of Canadian ownership, including the establishment of a federal agency to supervise the conduct of foreign-controlled operations in Canada, and in particular any new take-overs. We draw special attention to the early establishment of a Canada Development Corporation and the policy on sale of our energy resources.

2. To foster a national development program, we urge the greater allocation of resources — both private and public — to the less well developed regions of the country.

3. Safeguarding Canadian control as well as a reasonable amount of Canadian news and content in our newspapers, magazines, radio, television stations and cable TV networks should form an essential part of Government policy. Adequate financial support must be provided to achieve these objectives.

4. We are convinced that trade unions in Canada must have the autonomy necessary for them to reflect the aspirations of their Canadian membership.

5. Within their respective jurisdictions, governments at all three levels must become more active in the fight against pollution, even when cleaning up our environment infringes on established vested interests. This emphatically includes the protection of Canadian jurisdiction in our Arctic.

6. One of the most important functions of our educational institutions is to enhance our cultural life. This means that without in any way isolating ourselves from the benefits to be obtained abroad, there should be a reasonable degree of information about Canada in curriculum and a reasonable knowledge about Canada on the part of the members of the teaching personnel.

7. Since foreign policy is an extension of domestic policy, the objectives stated here should be reflected and supported in our relations with all other nations. A general foreign policy designed to ensure Canadian independence must be formulated by our Government and its implications followed through in our relations abroad.

We are convinced that a majority of Quebeckers prefer to remain within Confederation. With this the case, it is in the best interest of Quebec and Canada as a whole that we should work together to promote genuine independence for Canada.

The Committee for an Independent Canada has been created to enlist the support of all Canadians in urging their MP's and MLA's to make Canada's survival as an independent nation their top priority.

DATE DUE
DATE DE RETOUR